Jesus the teacher is so often misunderstood, and we in the churches have to take our share of responsibility for that. Congratulations to Mark for a wonderful new look at Jesus through educational eyes. *Jesus Christ, Learning Teacher* asks questions about how Jesus the teacher is presented to us in the text of the Gospels, and in the imagination and teaching of the contemporary churches. Bad theology costs lives. But in this book we have good, life-giving theology, good surprises about Jesus, and practical ways forward for the churches.

The Revd Steve Chalke MBE, Founder and Leader,
Oasis Global

An outstanding book, one that needed to be written. It has a strong foundation in scholarship and professional experience. Mark's argument that the church needs to take the educational Christ more seriously in its educational and pastoral work is topical and compelling.

Fr Richard Peers, Sub-Dean, Christ Church Oxford

The quality of writing is beautifully clear. The range of scholarship is impressive. It reveals and shares lifelong personal reflection, intimate with text and interpreters in the life of the church. It will speak to fellow Christians, especially those with links to formal education. Jesus, the real and learning teacher, comes clearly through the author's experience and reflection. The book is complete as it stands, and it builds symphonically.

Brian Gates MBE, Emeritus Professor of Religion, Ethics and Education, University of Cumbria

Jesus Christ, Learning Teacher

Where Theology and Pedagogy Meet

Mark Chater

scm press

© Mark Chater 2020

Published in 2020 by SCM Press
Editorial office
3rd Floor, Invicta House,
108–114 Golden Lane,
London EC1Y 0TG, UK
www.scmpress.co.uk

SCM Press is an imprint of Hymns Ancient & Modern Ltd
(a registered charity)

Ancient
&Modern

Hymns Ancient & Modern® is a registered trademark of
Hymns Ancient & Modern Ltd
13A Hellesdon Park Road, Norwich,
Norfolk NR6 5DR, UK

Biblical quotations are from The Jerusalem Bible, published and
copyright © 1966, 1967 and 1968 by Darton, Longman and
Todd Ltd and Doubleday, a division of Random House, Inc.
and used by permission.

978-0-334-05968-4

British Library Cataloguing in Publication data

A catalogue record for this book is available
from the British Library

Typeset by Regent Typesetting
Printed and bound by
CPI Group (UK) Ltd

Contents

This book is dedicated to the memory of
Professor John Hull, 1935–2015,
wise teacher, generous mentor, compassionate friend

Acknowledgements

This book has been with me on a long road, having started as a set of questions I was asking myself in mid-career about the relationship between the vocations of Christian educator and theologian. Many kind friends and colleagues have encouraged me along the way: their advice and their belief in the importance of this idea have sustained me. They include Tanya Ap Sion, Lat Blaylock, Bob Bowie, Alan Brine, Violet Brown, Steve Chalke, Philip Esler, Paul Fiddes, David Ford, Brian Gates, Beth Green, Gregory Hadley, Claire Henderson Davis, David Heywood, Danielle Lynch, Jürgen Moltmann, Fiona Moss, Richard Peers, Ros Stuart-Buttle, John Sullivan and Andrew Wright.

A note on the text

The biblical references are from the Jerusalem Bible, unless otherwise stated. God has no pronouns. The church is generic, unless a specific tradition, church or denomination is named.

Foreword

It is quite obvious really: of course Jesus learned to speak, to read, to pray, and so on, and Luke's Gospel gives a picture of him as a boy in the sort of intensive conversation ideal for learning. Of course Mary his mother was vital for his development. And of course he went on learning throughout his life. He has also been one of the most influential teachers ever. So how is he to be understood as a learning teacher?

One of the delights of this book is that it assumes there can be many worthwhile answers to that question, that there is no end to the inquiry, and that the reader is not being asked to agree with all the conclusions. Rather, the reader is being invited to explore a fascinating and important topic as the author leads by example. Mark Chater is both an experienced teacher and a well-educated and thoughtful theologian, and he has a deep desire for learning, for teaching, for truth, and for God. His writing above all seeks to arouse and intensify that desire in others. He does this with an attractive combination of modest, reflective autobiography going back to childhood, opening up something of his own spiritual and intellectual journey, together with a distillation of the educational and theological wisdom that he has gathered along the way.

Above all, his approach is imaginative, offering a vivid picture of Jesus as learner and teacher, and improvising on the Bible in order to bring home Jesus' immense contemporary relevance. I especially appreciated his fictional, pointed updating of the teaching of Jesus. Through all his daring interpretations of the Gospels there is also a surefootedness in his use of biblical scholarship. And I love the lasagne image: that the tradition has many layers, from the earliest testimonies to Jesus right down to today, and each of them has nourishing meat.

Of recent teachers in the tradition, the one who stands out is Chater's own teacher, the late John Hull, to whom the book is dedicated. I knew John well in Birmingham, where we were both members of a monthly theological and philosophical discussion group, during the years in which he was slowly going blind. It is very good indeed to savour in Mark Chater's work something of the taste of John Hull's provocative wisdom.

This book will be a gift to anyone involved in teaching about Jesus in any setting, but also, more than that, to anyone open to encountering Jesus afresh or for the first time.

David F. Ford
Regius Professor of Divinity Emeritus
University of Cambridge

Introduction: Jesus Christ, learning teacher – is that even possible?

Is Jesus Christ, the fully divine and fully human God-man of Christian teaching, believable? In his life, was he a real human being who learned as he lived? As a teacher, did he learn and grow, as all good teachers do? Or was he parachuted in with a predetermined mission? As a teacher and saviour, is he effective and accessible for us?

These questions matter to ordinary people inside the churches. In quite different ways, the questions are also live ones for those hanging on to Christianity by their eyelids, those who have left it, and those who have never belonged. For their sake, the questions should matter to Christian teachers and others in Christian ministry, and those who train or supervise them.

Churches have real difficulty in communicating to these groups, and close to the heart of the problem is the challenge of blending or combining Christ's divinity and his humanity. We have often assumed that a divine teacher, coming to earth, knows everything, needs to learn nothing, and in effect only appears to be human. Or we have tilted the other way and assumed that Christ's incarnation into humanity means that he sets aside his divinity in order to become like us. Both these positions, in the history of the church, are classed as heresies – a harsh word for the belief-choices that fail to capture the full complexity of the tradition. Adult lay Christians can struggle to articulate the tensions of this complexity, let alone resolve them. They inhabit a church where the awkward, creative tensions in theology, embedded in the Bible and tradition, are too seldom explored, so that problems lie neglected, gathering power in the darkness.

It is rare for qualified theologians to break into that darkness. One of them who did, Elizabeth Templeton, warned of an 'unhelpful collusion' between clergy who avoid airing difficult issues in their preaching – 'I mustn't disturb my people' – and laity who feel that their thoughts and questions lack legitimacy or decency – 'I can't say this out loud to the minister/priest'.[1] The recent studies of what is called 'ordinary theology'[2] have shown that the ways in which lay Christian church-goers think and talk about God are largely untouched by academic theology. The dream articulated by the theologian David Tracy – of theology as public conversation between society, the academy and church – is largely unrealized.[3] Lay Christians live daily with the contradictions of theology, but without the language to articulate them or place them in any perspective, and also without the power to access language or raise questions.

An enquiry into Jesus as teacher? Proceed with caution

When I as a teacher look at the teacher Jesus as reported in the Gospels and preached in churches, a number of issues confront me. The issues have occurred to me over a career spent as a Christian in education. They relate to the purpose and manner of his teaching, how his role as a teacher fits in with his other titles: Lord, Christ, Son of Man, Lamb of God, among others. They also relate to how the church has handled its memory of Jesus the teacher, and how effective we have been in conveying the complexity he presents, through the many layers of Gospel formation, redaction, interpretation and reception.

There can be two significant objections to this line of enquiry. The first, a doctrinal objection, is based upon the Christian reality of Jesus' lordship. Who am I to comment critically on Christ? Why do I – why do any of us – even need to ask what kind of teacher he was? Jesus the Christ is the first born of all creation, the image of God and the model of our humanity. Because he is the Christ, he was and is a good teacher, the best teacher. If we seek to teach well, we should model ourselves on him, rather than brandish our broken pedagogical apparatus at his perfect example. And yet I do not for a minute accept that Jesus' status as Son of God and saviour place him beyond critical enquiry. I write about this not in spite of my membership of Christ but because of it: faithfully, searchingly, aspiring to the truth and integrity that he showed.

A second objection to this project is epistemological and hermeneutical. What do I know about Jesus the teacher? I may think I know him very well. This can be as much a disability as a help; it makes me assume familiarity with, for example, his parables and conversations in the Gospels. I can still recall my dawning sense of clarity on realizing that much of the Gospel material on Jesus was not an eyewitness account, that early church oral traditions and editing had a strong hand in arranging the material. It was a realization carefully kept from me as a child; yet it offered me a way to make sense of textual contradictions that had long puzzled me. In preaching, we hardly ever hear rehearsed a critical treatment of the Gospels as literature – and what unique literature they are. It is easy to misunderstand and misuse the Gospels.

My response to these objections – which have accompanied me all the way, like reservations about a journey even after I have started out – has been to proceed with caution. An enquiry into Jesus as a teacher must dig into the Gospel material on Jesus' teaching with real care, taking nothing for granted, and respecting the limits of what we can and cannot know about him. In doing so, I must also be aware of my own context, and how difficult, probably impossible, it is to step outside it. Yet I must also use my pedagogical imagination to complete the incomplete picture of the teacher in the Gospels. The task of the chapters in Part 1 is to set in place some definitions – contestable ones, certainly – of what we can know, how we can manage our baggage, and how our disciplines of theology and pedagogy might work together, stimulating our imagination as Christians and educators.

Teacher or saviour?

The solemn Passiontide hymn 'Ride on, ride on in majesty' adopts a post-resurrection viewpoint from which it urges Jesus on to the cross and the triumph beyond it:

> Ride on, ride on in majesty!
> In lowly pomp ride on to die.[4]

In similar vein, Bach's *St John Passion* includes an aria urging oppressed souls to press on to Golgotha, the place of execution:

> Haste, haste, haste.
> Where? Where? Where?
> Come, come to Golgotha.[5]

If it feels awkward, perhaps even wrong or sadistic, to urge ourselves and Christ forward on the journey to a horrific death, we should pause and note our emotional response before rushing to justify it with theology. The theology at work in these and other passages of Christian music is a predetermined narrative in which the drama of sacrifice and salvation must be acted out. They press home a message that Christ's sacrifice is absolutely necessary, so we should glorify it and hasten towards it, rather than (as seems natural) shrink from it.

From this theology, that Jesus' sacrifice was always necessary and inevitable, there arise several interesting problems about the significance of his ministry of teaching and healing. How does Christian theology account for the violent climax of Jesus' teaching career? If Jesus' teaching was successful, why did its impact trigger a chain of events that led to his arrest and execution? Or if the cross was always the inevitable end point, what was the purpose of a three-year teaching ministry? The purpose could have been educational or salvific. Did he teach the disciples in order to deepen their understanding and commitment – something we would assume in any good teacher – or did he all along know that they would betray and deny, scatter and fail? When the Gospels portray Jesus as predicting that 'You will all lose faith in me this night',[6] apparently in fulfilment of an older prediction by the prophet Zechariah,[7] are we to place our confidence in a prophet of crisis or in a teacher of understanding?

This problem presents itself as a challenge not only to the *purpose* of Jesus' teaching but also to its *conduct*. At several moments, Jesus' teaching appears to be preprogrammed to fulfil a prophecy. For example, he left Nazareth and made his home in Capernaum, in 'the land of Zebulun and Naphtali, so that what had been spoken by the prophet Isaiah might be fulfilled'.[8] There often seems to be a disconnect between Jesus' desire to help people understand the kingdom and his destiny to fulfil Scripture by appearing in various places and then facing a sacrificial death. When the Gospels attempt to reconcile this tension, the effort seems forced:

> This is what I meant when I said, while I was still with you, that everything written about me in the Law of Moses, in the prophets and in the Psalms, has to be fulfilled.[9]

As a result of this unresolved tension, the overall message now is refracted, unstructured and fragmented. The synoptic Gospels show Jesus at first persuading, informing, inspiring, challenging; then they and the fourth Gospel show him meekly accepting a foreordained destiny on the cross. The resulting lack of coherence matters in several ways. We should be wary of theologies that 'isolate his death from his life-praxis and posit it alone as redemptive in itself'.[10] Missiologically, the separation damages the church's work when a teaching Jesus, whose methods and ethical messages command assent well beyond the church's boundaries, is interrupted by a sacrificial Christ whose death and resurrection are much harder to explain.

In salvific terms, the purpose of his teaching is far from clear, and seems redundant if the cross was always inevitable and necessary. In pedagogical terms, the passion narrative violently cuts across his teaching, and negates the promise of the kingdom which he taught with such passion. It is almost as if two books have been rudely forced together: the first half of a teaching Gospel, and the second half of a sacrifice Gospel, stapled to each other with the crude stitching of biblical prognostications apparently fulfilled.

Something of this literary misalliance, with its resulting awkwardness of plot structure, is hinted at by Philip Pullman's fictional thesis that Jesus was two people.[11] Pullman identified a dissociation between Jesus the teacher and his brother Christ the cynic. Into the gap between, he projected an imagined conflict in which Christ manipulates Jesus into becoming a sacrificial victim. Christian theological attempts to explain the dissociation between Jesus the teacher and Jesus the sacrifice tend to prioritize the sacrifice and distort the teaching: so Jesus' teaching was successful, but not so good as to persuade where it mattered; unsuccessful, but not so bad as to weaken his divine status. Even Kierkegaard becomes caught on the horns of this dilemma.[12] To a teacher, the irregularities and dissonances in this way of reading the Gospel accounts seem unconvincing and forced. They beg the question: why did he teach?

The Gospel accounts of Jesus are puzzling to a teacher. Alongside the great stories, they include mistakes, backtrackings, confrontations, exaggerations, unfair criticisms, and other apparent failings. Christians tend to overlook these facets of Jesus' teaching, or to explain them away. The obduracy of the crowd, and the evil intentions of the scribes and Pharisees, are very common explanatory strategies. But it is appropriate to get underneath these explanations and learn something from Jesus the at times apparently unsuccessful teacher. How good a teacher was he, really? Of course, there is also the question of how far the early Christian church, sifting and editing its material and memory, placed his teaching in specific contexts to make a point. Their memory of Jesus the teacher is the only record we have.

As a teacher I am interested in Jesus' teaching and planning mind, the origins and consistency of his content, the cognitive pain and shock evinced by his hearers, and their progress in understanding; and in the church's life as Christ's teaching and learning body. All these teaching realities, of which the Gospels say little, can be to some extent brought out, and can perhaps shed a little new light on who he was and is for us. The chapters in Part 2 all attempt to look into Jesus' planning and teaching mind.

A divine learner?

Good teachers are also learning; in what sense can we see Jesus as a learning teacher? Can the Son of God be a learner? To claim that the God-man was a learner goes straight to the heart of the difficulty of Jesus' two natures, as fully human and fully divine, and to its richness. And yet I believe that reflection on the learning Christ can help us with a fully orthodox understanding of his divinity, and of the Trinity.

At first sight, the impression given in the Gospels is that Jesus was the divine man who knew everything. The thinking verbs used of Jesus serve to reinforce a sense of his omniscience and superiority: Jesus, seeing ...; Jesus, knowing ...; Jesus, opening his mouth. How surprised we would all be if we opened a Gospel in which we read about: Jesus, discovering ...; Jesus, reasoning ...; Jesus, reflecting ...; Jesus, speculating ...; Jesus, realizing he had been wrong ... and so on. Yet I as a teacher bring to my reading of the Gospels a knowledge, born of experience and reflection, that to be a good teacher means to be a lifelong learner. The theologian Rudolf Bultmann was right to warn us that:

Many passages [in the fourth Gospel] ... represent Jesus as the 'divine man' in the Hellenistic sense – a man who has miraculous knowledge at his command, does miracles, and is immune to the plottings of his enemies.[13]

If the Gospels portray Jesus in this way, even more so do the non-canonical Gospels influenced by Gnosticism. There, Jesus is a child prodigy, full of divine knowledge from an early age, making it impossible to believe in his humanity in any recognizable way.[14] This Gnostic strain also found its way into Greek philosophy, from where it influenced the development of Christian doctrine. But we can turn away from our image of the authoritative, omniscient teacher, and seek instead a learning teacher who is more consistent with what we believe about Jesus' humanity, and what we know about teaching. To Bultmann's theological warning, John Hull, the theologian-educator whose work has influenced mine in this book, adds his perspective:

> Christ ... the authoritative and all-knowing teacher has certainly had more impact upon the church than Christ the questioning learner ... There are today many Christian people who still take it for granted that Jesus knew the future although the implications of this for his humanity are seldom drawn out. To be incapable of curiosity, surprise or disappointment, to be in principle incapable of undergoing cognitive development, to be unable to forget, all these characteristics would be such as to indicate not so much a human being as an alien creature. And yet, many Christians continue to believe that the divinity of Jesus is displayed in these very characteristics.[15]

And Hull warns that the theological construction of what he calls 'an unlearning Jesus'[16] is not faithful to the Gospel or the tradition. Yet *pace* Hull's acute critique, lay Christians should hardly be blamed for thinking this way about Jesus if their church has deprived them of the language and power needed to read the Gospels differently.

So how does today's church, the living embodiment of Christ, measure up to him as a learning teacher? Can we release our Christian and educational imagination when we reflect on Jesus the learning teacher? What would it mean to have a church that fully reflected the saviour's capacity to learn and to teach? If we were to prioritize educational dimensions more, would this in any way change our doctrine and practice? These questions are explored in Part 3.

From theology of education to educationalization of theology

Much has been written about Jesus the master teacher. In their Christian devotion, writers have held Jesus to be a faultless example of the teacher, challenging, inspiring, applicable to all contexts and times, including the western world in the twenty-first century.[17] Similarly, there has been prolific output on Christian theologies of education.[18] This book is not another of either of those; indeed it is written as an educator's response to both. It is an 'educationalization of theology',[19] which John Hull held to be essential in creating a conducive environment for Christians to grow and deepen their faith. Whereas studies of Jesus as a master teacher take his methodology uncritically and apply his approaches more or less directly to modern classrooms, I reverse the direction and apply an educator's questions and perspectives to the Gospel text and to the figure of Jesus as teacher. And whereas Christian theologies of education consider the relationship between an *a priori* Christian theological tradition, often making useful proposals on ministry, ecclesiology and faith development, I again reverse the direction by asking what impact an educator's Jesus might have on the tradition. Thus I am attempting an exploration of what a teaching perspective can bring to our understanding and love of Christ. I have written this in the belief that the way we see Jesus as a teacher, and the way we see ourselves, need re-examining; and that a teacher's lens – a learning teacher's lens – can be a powerful instrument for re-examination.

The book uses several approaches: biography, critical professional reflection, biblical study, systematic theology and practical theology. My teacher's instinct tells me that a multidisciplinary approach facilitates the moving forward of understanding on several fronts at the same time. Within parameters established by relevance, and the confines of space in one book, it is legitimate to change disciplines, bringing out of the storeroom things new and old.

Notes

1 Elizabeth Templeton, 2004, 'Theology as a Tool for Transformation', in Alastair Hulbert and Peter Matheson (eds), 2019, *In Your Loving is Your Knowing: Elizabeth Templeton: Prophet of our times*, Edinburgh: Birlinn Ltd, pp. 66–72, p. 69.

2 Jeff Astley and Leslie Francis (eds), 2013, *Exploring Ordinary Theology: Everyday Christian believing and the church*, Farnham, Surrey and Burlington, VT: Ashgate.

3 Stephen Okey, 2018, *A Theology of Conversation: An introduction to David Tracy*, Collegeville, MN: Liturgical Press.

4 Henry Milman, 'Ride on, ride on in majesty!' in Church of England, 1986, *New English Hymnal*, Norwich: Canterbury Press, Hymn 511.

5 Johann Sebastian Bach, 1981, *Johannes-Passion*, Basel, London and New York: Bärenreiter Kassel, pp. 42–150.

6 Matthew 26.30–31.

7 Zechariah 13.7.

8 Matthew 4.12–13.

9 Luke 24.44–45.

10 Francis Schüssler Fiorenza, 1975, 'Critical social theory and Christology: Toward an understanding of atonement and redemption as emancipatory solidarity', *Proceedings of the Catholic Theological Society of America* 30, pp. 63–110, pp. 101–2.

11 Philip Pullman, 2011, *The Good Man Jesus and the Scoundrel Christ*, Edinburgh and London: Canongate.

12 Howard V. Hong and Edna H. Hong (eds), 1985, *Søren Kierkegaard: Philosophical fragments*, Princeton, NJ: Princeton University Press, p. 11.

13 R. Bultmann, 1973, 'Theology of the New Testament', in E. Tinsley (ed.), *Modern Theology*, London: Epworth Press, pp. 121–37, p. 124.

14 Bart D. Ehrman and Zlatko Plese (eds), 2014, *The Other Gospels: Accounts of Jesus from outside the New Testament*, Oxford: Oxford University Press.

15 John Hull, 1985, *What Prevents Christian Adults from Learning?* London: SCM Press, pp. 204–6.

16 Hull, 1985, p. 206.

17 Roy Pitcher, 2013, *Jesus: A master teacher*, Bloomington, IN: Authorhouse UK Ltd; Bill Donahue, 2005, *Jesus: Provocative teacher*, Leicester: IVP; Robert Pazmino, 2001, *God our Teacher: Theological basis in Christian education*, Grand Rapids, MI: Baker Academic.

18 Randolph Crump Miller (ed.), 1995, *Theologies of Religious Education*, Birmingham, AL: RE Press; Leslie Francis and Adrian Thatcher (eds), 1990, *Christian Perspectives for Education: A reader in the theology of education*, Leominster: Fowler Wright Books; Jeff Astley and Leslie Francis (eds), 1996, *Christian Theology and Religious Education: Connections and contradictions*, London: SPCK; J. Estep, M. Anthony and G. Allison, 2008, *A Theology of Christian Education*, Nashville, TN: Broadman and Holman.

19 Hull, 1985, p. 209.

PART I

First born

I

A teacher looks at Jesus: Baggage and biography

Introduction

Why would a teacher, whose lifelong career has been in education, attempt to write a work of Christology? This particular teacher has a bachelor degree in theology and a doctorate in theology and education, but has published no academic theology and is not a New Testament scholar. Mainly what I bring to Christology is a set of questions that a Christian educator asks. The aetiology of those questions is autobiographical, and in as much as this chapter contains aspects of personal memory, this is not so much because of any intrinsic interest in my life story. It is more because of an intention to demonstrate how an educator regards theology, and how a Christian educator brings a particular and perhaps unexpected hermeneutic to the task of understanding and following Christ.

In looking at Jesus we all have hermeneutical baggage, which may become either a burden or a gift. That was what Milan Machovec, in his groundbreaking *A Marxist Looks at Jesus*,[1] a book I read as an undergraduate, taught me; it was as much about *method* in theology as it was about content. Later, work such as Kelly Brown Douglas's *The Black Christ*[2] and Marcella Althaus-Reid's feminist and queer hermeneutics in *Indecent Theology*[3] added to the tradition of bringing a particular identity to the study of Jesus – bringing it into the classroom, counting it as an enrichment of method, rather than being required to leave it outside in some doubtful attempt at the highly contestable notion of objectivity.

3

A teacher's baggage is as particular as anyone else's. Here is mine.

Some cognitive strands of Christian identity

Like most Christians, I do not consciously remember my own baptism. Despite its seismic significance in re-creating me as a child of God, participating in Christ's death and resurrection, and inducting me on my first steps as a member of his church, nothing at all of the actual event stays with me. The certificate in my files is a cold record for such a vital event. In so far as I carry around any baptismal thoughts, they are related to the ritual I've seen countless times as an adult, for which I've helped to prepare parents, and witnessed being administered to their children. My own children, and the children of members of the parishes I've belonged to, are heirs of a ritual that I too received; they go through the same portal, and in so doing bring to mind the door that was opened to me. The identity conferred on them confirms mine. My understanding of baptism grew through their experience of it, not directly through my own.

In the middle-of-the-road Church of England parishes of my childhood and adolescence, the hymns we sang taught me a strange thing. Those that stirred me most deeply were 'Immortal, invisible', closely followed by 'O worship the King, all glorious above'. Others in my juvenile ecclesiastical hit parade included 'Lord enthroned in heavenly splendour'. What I have slowly realized throughout my Christian life is that those hymns all have in common a rich theological language coupled with a poetic restraint, a treading-around who God might be, that is sometimes called the *via negativa* or apophatic theology. The hymns achieve this through a number of stylistic mannerisms: by singing of what God is not, or by dwelling on how it is impossible for us to see God directly, or by heaping associated glory on that which is proximate to God, because God's self cannot be glimpsed or described. Yet the language is not facile: the focus is still on God, not on how we feel about God.

As a child, singing the limits of human knowing, I was gazing right into the divine mystery. The power of the apophatic – 'measureless might, ineffable love',[4] 'though the lowliest form doth veil thee'[5] – drew me ever more deeply into the mystery, as if it were a drama. And the colourful language lavished on the proximates – 'his chariots of wrath the deep thunder clouds form, and dark is his path on the wings of the storm',[6] 'stricken rock with streaming side'[7] – paradoxically hid the divine splendour while also enabling me to intuit why it was hidden, yet still sense it. The metaphorical language, even when elaborate, was never a barrier. I did not understand the metaphors cognitively, and felt no need to. They exercised a gravitational pull towards a mysterious, enthralling, beautiful centre. In cultural terms I owe my lifelong desire for Christ to the poets and composers of the eighteenth and nineteenth centuries, and to the clergy who selected their hymns Sunday after Sunday.

There were daily and weekly religious routines set by my parents, both of them middle-class lay people. My mother taught me the words of prayers – the Our Father and the General Confession. My father wept in church sometimes, quietly, particularly on Good Fridays. I watched their sincere and unassuming faith practice, which they both kept up all their life, and observed it deepening as they reached old age. They could laugh gently over the church's foibles, and they could be hurt when it let them down. They had some theological questions – the problem of evil came up regularly – but no theological language and no formal theological education. They relied mainly on institutions and formulas, but were no less genuine for it, and no less profound. The spiritual debt I owe them is for their lifelong habits of unashamed piety and their loving tolerance.

The other key influence was my aunt and godmother, who took the family's middle-class Anglicanism and transplanted it in African soil – or, better, rediscovered and redefined it there. For 60 years she lived as a member of an African Christian community in Zimbabwe. The four prolonged visits I made there, between the ages of 18 and 55, gave me religious experiences of strangeness and familiarity. The liturgy and hymns were English, the language and way of singing was Shona, the spirituality Catholic and ancestral. In that (to me) strange culture I found the familiar convictions both revealed and occluded, the jewel of faith turning in her hand and glinting with new lights.

I experienced baptism long before I understood it; I rejoiced in treading the *via negativa* long before I knew what the words meant or how the language was formed; I sensed my parents' untutored faith and followed their routines long before I studied it academically or lived it existentially; and I glimpsed how culture lays a palimpsest over religious insight, now disclosing, now effacing. Because of this experience, I am grateful to all the adults – the pastors, composers, educators, and my family – who have given me substantial theology and have held back from trying to tell me everything. The adults around me, including in parish and school, exercised that self-restraint with fidelity. The trust they placed in the power of rich language and repeated ritual, their poetic delicacy in pointing to a mystery without presuming to define it neatly, and above all their trusting in time, life experience and divine providence to guide me along, now seem to be hallmarks of rich, responsible and respectful theological education in practice. On the whole, they avoided the twin mistakes of condescension – making it all too simple, too nice, too child-centred – and overexplanation – attempting to explain and qualify every ritual act, every puzzling text. Others have been less fortunate than me: those twin mistakes are very visible in many contemporary churches and schools.

Only twice have I embraced theologies of absolute certainty. Both occasions were intense conversion experiences, once in my late teens to evangelicalism, the other in my late twenties to Roman Catholicism. On both occasions the spell of certainty was short-lived, as the questions and ambiguities came crowding back in, like old friends seeking to reconnect with me, clamouring to enrich and complicate my life. Those two periods of certainty now seem like inoculations: today, whenever I visit a church or meet a Christian wrapped in their own certainty, I find little to attract me and much to cause alarm.

Other than those times, my Christian life has been one of incremental revelation: learning, forgetting, learning again a little more deeply; moving through cycles of arrogance and humility; having my angle of vision shifted by infinitesimal nudges, so that I would see a text or a ritual differently – a cycle made of small steps, very familiar to educators,[8] and also to mystics.[9]

Over time, I have learnt that God in Christ is both knowable and unknowable to us: a state of affairs described in Jewish and Christian Scripture.[10] In the same way, any good teacher is both clear and opaque to learners. This, I think, is how we are drawn onwards. The only way by which theology moves and people receive new revelations is by learning. Revelation can change learning but cannot bypass it.

Christian and teacher identity

That theology is one tangled skein, in which the beginnings and endings are hard to find and the journey full of twists and knots, has been a repeated lesson. Reading the Bible as a teenager, it was so easy to latch on to a sentence and act out a mono-focal relationship to that bit of text, for fear of endless confusion. At the very edge of my vision, prodding but never speaking, was a question that I could not even articulate: how does all this fit together? How does grace fit with sin? How do miracles and the kingdom make a difference here, now? The questions did occasionally throw me off course; what brought me back was ritual, habit, and later submitting to the disciplinary yoke of theology.

Theology at university gave me the gift of applying questions in an organized way and knowing that others had been there before. I knew that fundamentalist certainty had nothing more to give me when I heard its exponents pitying me for studying theology and warning me that it might damage my faith. In doing so they had played a card that revealed the weakness of their hand. In God's dispensation, the complexities of theology, the perils of trying to understand, no matter how frightening they might be, could never separate us from the love of God.

That skein had a subtle unity that kept slipping into and out of view. In my final year, some fellow students and I were by then on friendly enough terms with a few of our tutors to be able to discuss theology informally with them, and one evening we met up over a drink. Our faculty of theology was then divided into five departments: Old Testament, New Testament, ecclesiastical history, systematic theology, and practical theology with Christian ethics. It was a deeply conventional arrangement, long since reorganized (this was the early 1980s). In our studies we imbibed mainly from systematic theology and ecclesiastical history, but in our spare time we read liberation theology: feminist, Latino, and emerging black and queer theologies. We wanted to ask our tutors: how is it that we learn about the social dimensions of the kingdom in Christian ethics? Why do we not learn about them in systematic theology and church history? How is it that we learn about the uses and misuses of Scripture in practical theology, instead of encountering them as hermeneutical problems in Old and New Testament? Essentially we were asking for a liberationist reconstruction of theology, enacted through a reorganization of the faculty. It was a perfectly amicable discussion. One of our tutors said, 'I agree with you', but then, 'It will never happen'. That evening I learnt something about the theological structures that exist inside the minds of Christians, and how difficult it is to question the structures in the academy or the church, let alone change them.

My entry into the teaching profession was both accidental and foreseeable. At the time it felt like an accident: something that would earn me a living until a truer vocation manifested itself. Looking back, it was certainly foreseeable, perhaps even little short of inevitable, that someone whose life had received the imprint of questions and answers, and a fascination with knowing and not knowing, should find his way into teaching. So I came to my second identity.

Teachers' worlds can be like the Gospel world. Teachers have their call-narratives, their miraculous moments of professional self-realization, and encounters or episodes that change their professional view for ever. Teachers are praised, welcomed, tested, rejected, crucified. Teachers are everywhere in Jesus' stories, hiding in plain view. The attractive and noble characters who populate the Gospels – Son of Man figures, like Daniel, taming the beast and keeping people safe; compassionate shepherds, searching for the hundredth sheep; extravagantly generous vineyard owners, good Samaritans, persistent women, watchful servants, wise bridesmaids who keep the light burning – are people in whom we can glimpse the teachers we have met, or even the teachers we are. There are the less noble characters, too – stiff-necked elder brothers, grumbling vineyard workers, stern judges, unforgiving debtors, those who will not go through the door and will not allow others to – and a very interesting handful of the ambiguous – the fickle crowd, susceptible to rumour, the cautious Nicodemus, the uncertain Governor – who are also recognizable among our teacher colleagues. And there are so many symbolic objects – yeast, lamp, seed on rocky ground, seed on rich soil. Sometimes our professional identity can house several of these characters and objects all at once. All these characters and objects are sanctified by their encounter with Christ. Christian educators could perhaps afford to be more confident than we are in seeing how the many professional identities that we carry around inside ourselves – a legion – can each be blessed and redeemed.

Theological ideas in the minds of learners

Among the many good things that teaching taught me, I learnt that competent teachers stand on the most important spot in the room. Physically, it is the spot where they can see and be seen, hear and be heard; psychologically, it is the exact place between the idea studied and the minds and capacities of the learners. The prolific educationalist Lev Vygotsky called this space the 'zone of proximal development',[11] meaning the zone of culture or curriculum in which learners cannot absorb an idea on their own, but can encounter it meaningfully with the intervention of a teacher – if the teacher is standing in the space and doing what the space requires. The space between a theological idea and the mind of a learner is a sacred space, too often neglected or invaded.

Neglect can happen through condescension, and invasion through overexplanation. Like many educators, I observe the condescension with which some pastors and teachers try to keep it nice for their learners, particularly for children. The garden of Eden without nakedness, the flood without drownings, Israel without conquest, even Easter without violent death – all these I have seen. But the Bible is not 'nice' and neither is God. The work of Robert Coles[12] reminds us that stories are a key way in which children can encounter evil safely. Most children, we hope, will have their first encounter with evil through a story, before they meet it directly. A story is a safe yet vivid way to see threat or jeopardy and the harm it can do. But if the stories told to children are all nice, if most of the evil, destructiveness and moral ambiguity is removed (whether through a desire to safeguard children or through a teacher's wish to elicit positive responses to the Bible), then the story is likely to feel dull, and the tradition as a whole will feel a little less interesting. This mistake evacuates the sacred space between the learner's mind and the theological ideas. Left empty, little grows there.

Overexplanation is the opposite mistake. The teacher or pastor, scrupulously conscious of how complex theology and ritual, text and doctrine can be, may be driven to give too much, invading the sacred space. A priest friend of mine used to rage against overexplanation. In bitter and accurate mimicry of his fellow clergy he would intone: 'This is a candle. A candle is a symbol of light. What does light do for us? Hands up? Yes, it lights up our house. But what does it remind us of? Anyone? Yes, it reminds us that Christ is the light of the world, the light shining in darkness.' Many times I have noticed how the compulsion to spell it all out is bad for the space, and therefore bad for the intrinsic power of rituals and texts. I have learnt that over-explanation weakens the audience, whether they are children or adults, because it atrophies their muscle for responding intuitively to symbols and for working on tough texts.

These mistakes – condescension and overexplanation – I too have made, many times, just as my colleagues have.

In addition to teaching children in schools, and later, teachers in universities, I was a voluntary adult theological educator. That this was the knottiest strand in my skein – often the least rewarding, though sometimes moving and miraculous – has often made me think of Christ and his crowds. In learning theology, adults in parishes experience their own barriers to understanding. The theological structures inside their minds have become less mobile than children's: more solid, yet paradoxically more vulnerable, even brittle, and less flexible. So, while their minds are better fitted for complexity, their literary toolbox more ready for tough texts, emotionally they will sometimes shy at the fences or kick away the feed bucket. Sometimes we have to admit the church's responsibility: perhaps a long-term diet of theologically lightweight preaching, of hymns or songs having little or no theological content, or a culture in which questioning and exploring faith is discouraged, may have unfitted the adults for complexity. The paddock, the theological enclosure, has the comfort of familiarity and safety. John Hull had much to say about adults, about their need to be right, and their sense of risk and pain involved in theological learning.[13] His approach to the problem was primarily psychological, whereas mine has been mainly educational, becoming theological.

Christian identity and teacher identity have followed each other, quarrelled with each other and made up, dozens of times in my story and hundreds of times in the history of the church. Within the educational endeavour of the church, different strands – *paideia* (education), *didache* (instruction) and *catecheo* (hearing, echoing, handing on) – have twisted around each other to form the theological skein and compete with each other for priority, and this is observable historically in both liberal protestant and catholic traditions of education.[14]

An academic colleague of mine has confessed that when he is with theologians he tends to emphasize his educational passions, and vice versa when with educationalists. I entirely sympathize with this habit; like my colleague, I occupy a liminal territory between Christian theology and education. When I read about Jesus in the Gospels, I experience him as an educator: placing myself in the story, I am either his pupil, or his colleague, or someone learning to teach like him, or (more rarely) someone quietly observing and thinking about his effectiveness. In my reading and interpretation I have not raced ahead to the empty tomb, to justify everything he said, as some Christians do. I am consciously adapting the Ignatian method of placing myself in the story of Jesus. The self I place there is a teacher – a planning, explaining, questioning, classroom-scanning, understanding-checking, curriculum-developing, colleague-supporting presence in the crowds. So the baggage that I bring to reading Jesus is pedagogical and andragogical baggage.

In my approach to writing this book, my interest is mainly in questions about knowledge and understanding: how Jesus worked with theological ideas; how the ideas grew in him, the inner dialogues he might have had; how he worked to enable growth in others; why and how he was sometimes successful as a teacher and sometimes not; what we as teachers, and as theologians, can learn in our own time from his successes and failures; and how the church can embrace the learning teacher, or betray him.

My professional hunch is that Jesus, seen as a teacher, is greatly more complex than we have usually assumed; but entering this complexity, we are rewarded with fresh insights into his identity as Christ. Where Christology meets pedagogy and andragogy, all these disciplines can be renewed.

Notes

1 Milan Machovec, 1976, *A Marxist Looks at Jesus*, Minneapolis, MN: Fortress Press.

2 Kelly Brown Douglas, 2019, *The Black Christ*, 25th anniversary edn, Maryknoll, NY: Orbis Books.

3 Marcella Althaus-Reid, 2000, *Indecent Theology: Theological perversions in sex, gender and politics*, London: Routledge.

4 Robert Grant, 'O worship the King all glorious above', in Church of England, 1986, *New English Hymnal*, Norwich: Canterbury Press, Hymn 433.

5 G. H. Bourne, 'Lord, enthroned in heavenly splendour', in Church

of England, 1986, *New English Hymnal*, Norwich: Canterbury Press, Hymn 296.

6 Grant, Hymn 433.

7 Bourne, Hymn 296.

8 Patrick Devitt, 1991, *How Adult is Adult Religious Education?* Dublin: Veritas, pp. 219ff.

9 Teresa of Avila, ET 1957, *The Life of Saint Teresa of Avila*, Harmondsworth: Penguin.

10 Isaiah 45.15; 1 Corinthians 13.12.

11 Harry Daniels, Michael Cole and James Wertsch (eds), 2007, *The Cambridge Companion to Vygotsky*, Cambridge: Cambridge University Press, pp. 276ff.

12 Robert Coles, 1989, *The Call of Stories: Teaching and the moral imagination*, Boston, MA: Houghton Mifflin Company; 1990, *The Spiritual Life of Children*, Boston, MA: Houghton Mifflin Company.

13 John Hull, 1985, *What Prevents Christian Adults from Learning?*, London: SCM Press, pp. 89ff.

14 Joseph Butler, 1962, *Religious Education: The foundations and practice of nurture*, New York: Harper and Row; Robert Ulich, 1968, *A History of Religious Education: Documents and interpretations from the Judaeo-Christian tradition*, New York: New York University Press; John H. Westerhoff III (ed.), 1981, *A Faithful Church: Issues in the history of catechesis*, Wilton, CT: Morehouse-Barlow.

2

A teacher looks at the church: Hermeneutics and education

Introduction

When I think about how the church teaches and preaches about Christ, how it portrays Christ as a true teacher, and how it presents theology, I am puzzled. This chapter tells two true stories that frame the problem. They are true both in the sense that they actually happened, although names and locations have been omitted, and because they truthfully speak to the Christian church's current unease about learning theology. These episodes took place recently in the UK, and if these stories resonate, in their different ways, this may be because they show churches that appear to have little strategy for thinking about Jesus as a teacher, whether in public or in private, or for thinking educationally about theology.

Myth vs fact

The first story concerns public communication of Christianity's central truth: the resurrection of Jesus from the dead. The problem is one of apologetics on the radio. We are waking on Easter morning, and the whole church is living the joyful culmination of the passion: the tomb is empty, and the risen Lord has been seen by some of his disciples. Anyone listening, Christian or not, might be seized by a sense that in God's dispensation, the gruesomeness of injustice, tyranny, torture and death are not the final word. On public service radio, a senior church leader with a strong academic background delivers a three-minute homily. He says that Jesus' resurrection from the dead is 'not a myth, it is a fact' – objective and real, forming the very basis of Christian belief and commitment.

Yet when I heard the words, 'not a myth, but a fact', I winced. The separation of myth from fact was not exactly subtle. It was as if the speaker wanted to ram home a message, without consideration for understanding, without patience or nuance, like a brute teacher, without exemplification of intelligence or respect for the vast tradition of theology, let alone the younger tradition of religious studies – all of which can inform our understanding of myth and history, if we allow them. Was he unaware of the significance myth plays in religion? Did he assume that we can only derive significance and meaning from historical events, or that the deepest and most powerful meanings are sourced in absolutely reliable histories? Was he afraid of *Daily Mail* headlines – 'Senior bishop calls Jesus' resurrection a myth' – and a subsequent summons to attend a doctrine panel? Or was he worried about denuding the people of their faith, in the fear that 'once you start stripping away, you finish up with very little'?[1] He was a senior church figure with considerable educational experience. Did he, then, hand over his rich and complex understanding of Jesus, betraying it into the hands of the dualists?

Next we are in a large church on the first day of a new school year. The entire cohort of first-year pupils in a church secondary school are gathered, fresh-faced and eager to learn, to please, to fit in. An ordained chaplain addresses them and asks how many have heard of the story of Adam and Eve. All hands go up. Next the priest asks how many of them think the story is true – that it actually happened. Nearly all hands go up: the children are 11 years old, and this is a church school. 'Well,' says the priest, 'it isn't true. In fact, it's a myth.' And he leaves the issue there with no explanation or questioning.

In some ways this is the same problem as the senior cleric on the radio, but approached from the other end of the false duality of myth vs fact. So we should ask similar questions. Why did the priest say that Adam and Eve was a myth, and leave it at that? There was something brutal about his stripping away of the outer layers of belief without providing any alternative garments. Perhaps the priest had engaged with critical readings of the biblical text, and took them seriously. Perhaps he was aware of the difficulties involved in leading young people's minds through the process of understanding how to read the Bible critically. Looking back on his own theological learning, reliving the twists and turns of wondering how revelation and critical apparatus could be negotiated and reconciled, remembering friends whose faith had withered under the glare of textual criticism, perhaps he became daunted by the dangers on the way he had come. In fearing that the journey of lifelong learning in theology is long and difficult, he was not wrong: it is a lifelong and life-changing journey,[2] it is hard, and it needs encouragement and protection.[3] Perhaps he did not trust the journey; perhaps he opted to take those children direct to the destination – his destination; fearful of the learning along the way and how complex and perilous it could be, perhaps he decided to take them straight to the conclusion – his conclusion. This fearfulness looks only to Christ at the end of the learning journey, and misses his presence *in* the learning journey. Was the priest, at that moment, in company with Peter, denying knowing his Lord in a dangerous place?

The learning journey and the loss of educational nerve

The twin failures of betrayal and denial are not of individuals alone: they are also a behaviour around the life and passion of Christ, repeated by the wider church in its struggle to accept and trust in Christ as a learning teacher, a God-man. No learning journey was opened up by either speaker. In their different ways, they both suffered from a loss of educational nerve. Their audiences suffered too.

To avoid being too harsh, we might speculate a little more about the background. Perhaps the radio speaker considered that in a three-minute slot on the church's most important feast day it would be necessary to be hard-hitting, definite and unambiguous; perhaps he saw 'not a myth, but a fact' as a clear note of certainty and faith to those who attended church but also entertained doubts, or as a clarion call to those who had wandered away. It is certain that he intended the homily to be helpful, both to those in the church and to those who are not. The priest addressing the 11-year-olds perhaps had little training in educational work, as this is not a normal part of ordination courses. It is possible to speculate that he intended to address them in a way that they would find intellectually stimulating, to set the tone for their career in school. Perhaps he wanted to challenge the notion that religion is composed of incredible stories. Perhaps, aware of how adolescence is a period in which childhood certainties are often questioned, he wanted to show them a less childish, more sophisticated understanding of the biblical text, one that they could relate to as they grew in mind and spirit. It is possible that these factors were in his mind when he told them that Genesis 1 didn't really happen.

However, this is speculation. What is more clear is that both speakers fell into an unexamined assumption of false duality, that truth must always be based on objective historical or scientific fact – a widespread perception of reality analysed by philosophers of the mind[4] – and a resultant belief that myth and truth are mutually exclusive opposites. It is a trap that catches many public communicators on religion, ensnaring both them and their listeners. It leads to impoverished theological understanding in the pews, of the sort described by researchers in ordinary theology.[5] These examples were failures not only of apologetics but of educational strategy. The Jesus they were trying to present was himself a teacher, yet they delved very little into his significance in educational terms.

Here we have heard two examples of a deep failure of educational nerve and apologetical strategy. This is a repeated problem in many churches. The learning Christ is a precious gift entrusted to his people. Betrayal and denial are at the crux of the tension between theology and education.

The theologian Paul Laffan recounts how he was protected as a child from any teaching of critical readings of the biblical text, only to have the truth of critical approaches revealed to him as an undergraduate by tutors who slowly and shame-facedly applied the necessary tools. Laffan described his sense of shock, but:

> I should be clear that the shock was not that of lost belief. It was moral ... Something had gone deeply wrong here: there was a complete disconnect between the higher reaches of re-search into the historicity of the Gospels and the preaching and teaching of Christianity.[6]

Have we, as a church, betrayed our divine teacher, denied his complexity and power? Have we blocked the path to learn-ing for others? Have we been so afraid of the complexities of a critical reading of Jesus as teacher that we abandon the attempt? Rudolf Bultmann advises preachers on integrity:

> The preacher in his sermons must not leave his hearer in any uncertainty as to what he requires them to believe to be true, in the strict sense of that term. Above all he must not leave the hearers in any uncertainty as to what he himself has suppressed; and in this regard he is bound to be completely honest with himself also.[7]

If this injunction seems addressed mainly to our first story, in other words to those preachers and teachers who deny or ignore a critical approach, then perhaps a second injunction in the same spirit might apply to the other case, to those who embrace critical readings but short-cut the complicated learning journey:

> Today's preacher must not leave her followers unclothed without any sense of what is true and essential. Crucially, she must not in the name of theology strip her hearers of their beliefs. She must look honestly at the twists and turns in her own learning journey in theology, and be guided by that when preparing others for theirs.

Conclusion

Understanding Jesus as a learning teacher does something for us as teachers. It opens up insights into the text of the Bible, and breathes air into Christian and educational imagination. It informs our own teaching and the values that underpin it. It restores our educational courage and strengthens our apologetics. And it does something deeply orthodox and radical for our doctrinal structures and our ways of understanding and doing theology.

Notes

1 Ann Christie, 2012, *Ordinary Christology*, Burlington, VT and Farnham: Ashgate, p. 79.

2 Margaret Cooling, 2005, *Creating a Learning Church: Improving teaching and learning in the local church*, London: Bible Reading Fellowship.

3 Frances Ward, 2005, *Lifelong Learning: Theological education and supervision*, London: SCM Press.

4 John R. Searle, 2015, *Seeing Things as They Are: A theory of perception*, Oxford: Oxford University Press.

5 Christie, 2012.

6 Paul Laffan, 2019, *The Fabricated Christ: Confronting what we know about Jesus and the Gospels*, Minneapolis, MN: Fortress Academic Press, pp. 1–2.

7 Rudolf Bultmann, quoted in Stephen Neill and Tom Wright, 1988, *The Interpretation of the New Testament 1861–1986*, Oxford: Oxford University Press, p. 242.

3

The dance of theology
and pedagogy

Introduction

When we look at Jesus the teacher, we hope not only to learn more about him but to adjust the relationship between the academic disciplines of theology and education. Specifically, the disciplines that could benefit are theology about the person and work of Christ, called Christology, and theory about teaching and learning, referred to as pedagogy. The relationship between Christology and pedagogy at the moment is unsatisfactory because one partner dominates and the other is subjugated. Theology and Christology, which deal in the hard currency of revealed eternal truth, can usually enforce their will on Christian education, as well as dictate the terms of debate in wider educational systems. This imbalance exists not only in the academy but also in churches, house groups and schools. We should make a distinction between the lively and discursive academic discipline of theology and the official theologies of churches. Neither of them is particularly successful in reaching the public, but official theologies have taken on the additional handicap of inflexibility in content and method.

Pedagogy is a child of many parents, among them psychology, sociology, culture, neuroscience, philosophy and theology. In strict linguistic terms it refers to the preparation of children for learning, but in educational settings the word is used generically to cover learners of any age. In this book I am interested in the learning of children and adults. Instead of referring repeatedly to pedagogy and andragogy, I shall use pedagogy in its generic sense as 'the act of teaching together with its attendant discourse about learning, teaching, curriculum and much else'.[1] When applied to Jesus as a teacher, the term can encompass both his acts of teaching and the ways in which he thought about his teaching. When applied to the church's theory and practice of education, the notable contrast is that whereas theology tends to deal in unchanging truths, pedagogy is critical and dynamic.[2] This chapter will argue that the demarcation of expertise between theologians and educators needs to move. It needs to become a dance of equal partners.

Pedagogy and theology in conflict

Let us take a particular example of domination and subjugation, and learn some principles from it. In 2012 a trainee teacher and Catholic, identifying as a gay man, expressed his deep sadness and concern about the Roman Catholic Church's campaign in schools against gay marriage. In a letter he wrote:

> I am only too aware of the power teachers have to shape the ideas and beliefs of the young people in their care. With this power comes responsibility, and I believe it irresponsible to present ideas against equality to schoolchildren ... I can only hope common sense prevails, with schools choosing not to peddle the church's campaign in this way.[3]

In setting his own educational principles against the doctrines of his church, the trainee teacher was not alone. Educators have found themselves in tension or conflict with religious authorities. It is noteworthy that his personal sense of calling as an educator impelled him to sign up to values, such as equality and (by implication) compassion, that placed him in conflict with the position of the church authorities.

It is rewarding to read his words carefully. His appeal to 'common sense' implies that the educational position, not the doctrinal one, is self-evidently correct; his hope that Catholic schools will abide by the former rather than the latter is an expectation that theology should and can change in the face of educational wisdom.

Perhaps similar conflicts enmeshed Jesus; perhaps the Jesus of our educational imaginings can be recreated, as good theology too rarely does, so that he embodies and even resolves those dilemmas. Educators who find themselves agreeing with the trainee teacher might wish to affirm their belief that education is about change, and that communities, insights into truth, people themselves, and yes, even doctrines, can change.

Except that they don't. The letter-writer and his colleagues have to choose between their educational convictions and the juggernaut of unquestionable doctrinal truth. This is a choice forced on them, not one of their seeking. Education in the churches is too often 'a story about the strategic compromises we make without even realizing it, the regimes to which we unknowingly and knowingly submit, and the tiny untruths we uncomfortably tell so that we can maintain relations'.[4]

This is more than one teacher's experience. A pattern exists whereby theology, the dominant partner, crowds out pedagogy, and pedagogy allows this to happen. This crowding-out takes several regular forms in churches. Writing from within the Catholic Church and the well-established discipline of research in Catholic education, Ros Stuart-Buttle remarks on the disconnection between theology and pedagogy. Recognizing the importance of pedagogy, she identifies serious weaknesses in teachers' biblical literacy, and draws lessons on the way training and formation are conceptualized.[5] In ministerial formation, pedagogical knowledge is often an overlooked ingredient, taking second place to theological content. It is seen as an option for some, which entirely misses the significance of studying how children and adults receive and process theological ideas. In churches and schools, pedagogical identity and aims are divergent between hierarchical leaders and school leaders, and between school leaders and front-line teachers. There is a complacent view that teaching is central to the church's mission, and that religious education is central to teaching. But it is not generally followed through in money spent, or in recognition of disciplinary and professional strength or status. What is needed is a rebalancing of theology and pedagogy, a new recognition of and respect for teaching and the teacher's mind, and a new humility and openness to allowing teachers and children to interrogate theology.

As they dance, it is always theology that leads and pedagogy that follows. Can we change the relationship between them? Can there be new steps in the old dance?

Changing the relationship

If we seek to change the power relationship between theology and pedagogy, both disciplines will be asked to make sacrifices in order to adjust their internal thought structures. In the case of Christology, the assumptions about Jesus as a master teacher or omniscient being will need to be re-evaluated, while for pedagogy, superficial parallels between teachers and Christ need to be left behind.

Jesus in the Gospels is both far less and far more than a teacher. He is less than a teacher because the Gospel narrative pays scant attention to his teaching craft. He seems to take little trouble to organize learning or set out a syllabus. He speaks sometimes plainly and sometimes with deliberate obscurity, loses patience with his learners, insults them, predicts their failure. He fails to convince the authorities of his right to teach. Placing too much of himself and his identity at the core of his teaching, he appears at times to be an egotistical teacher.

If we make these judgements about him, it is only because the Gospel accounts offer such poor evidence of him in this educational regard. As remembered accounts, they are fragmentary. As preaching material, they keep Jesus' thinking mind in the background, evidenced only by its resultant sayings and questions. We realize that insights into Jesus' teaching mind are not the primary purpose of the Gospels. Jesus the interpreter of people, the learner, the planner, is kept largely off stage. For these reasons, we note that the Jesus of the Gospels is less than a good teacher, even though there is some evidence of an educated and educating mind at work – a suppressed theme of the Gospels that we will explore in Part 2.

He is far more than a teacher, though, because he is the word of God, and in Christian theology this word breaks in on his followers in all ages to the present. In his own person he is both the revealer and the revelation. While it is true that Jesus encourages his followers to understand a Jewish Scripture that appears as a given, in the same way that a teacher opens up a body of pre-existing knowledge, it is also true that Jesus is himself the knowledge. This so explodes our notion of being a teacher as to make a dialogue between theology and pedagogy, as equal partners, a difficult enterprise. Pedagogy can help Christology to navigate through this problem by asking a teacher's questions about the Gospel record and about the church's mission.

Pedagogy is also called on to make sacrifices. One such letting go is pedagogy's image of itself in popular culture. In the 1989 film *Dead Poets Society*, a young-ish teacher of English is appointed to a private boarding school and gradually finds himself in conflict with its traditional values. The conflict deepens into tragedy and the teacher is sacked. Whatever one's views of the film, or the methods of the teacher, it is significant as one of several influencers in any dialogue between pedagogy and Christology. Central to the film's story is what we can call the crucified teacher theme.

The crucified teacher is shorthand for a cultural theme involving some apparent resemblances to Christ: the gifted and idealistic teacher who arrives from nowhere into a new environment; the struggle he or she has to achieve miracles with learners; the wonder evoked by new insights he or she opens up for them; the gradually emerging conflict with authorities; the betrayal; the expulsion; and, sometimes, the vindication. Other examples in fiction and film include *To Sir with Love*, *Stand and Deliver*, *Dangerous Minds*, *Freedom Writers* and *Mona Lisa Smile*. More interesting, because they are morally ambiguous, are the central characters in *The Prime of Miss Jean Brodie* and *The History Boys*. Although the crucified teacher is mainly a fictional construct, it has seeped its way into the professional culture of teaching. Individual teachers are sometimes portrayed as moral subjects caught up in a system that has forced bureaucratic and business values on them;[6] the entire state education system is sometimes written up in terms of victimhood, the culprits usually being neo-liberal politicians.[7] In the religious sphere of education, the celebrated Parker J. Palmer laments that educators 'are in real pain'[8] because they feel disconnected from their colleagues and from the system. This is not to deny the pain or alienation of some teachers; but it has been written up into a major theme, taking the form of a master story about teaching being a martyred profession.

These master stories owe a debt – usually unacknowledged – to the story of Jesus, and also to Socrates. But the resemblance is skin-deep. The complexity of the Gospels, their power of characterization and their use of symbol, are usually absent from these modern echoes. Any salvific effect, which in the Gospels is cosmic and universal, tends to be reduced. In the films, salvation comes on an individual and emotional scale; in works of educational criticism, it comes as exceeding expectations or as policy change. Pedagogy can and should dig deeper in its search for its points of dialogue with Christology.

The old shoes: how theology needs to be emancipated by pedagogy

If theology allows itself to be influenced by pedagogy – in the dance, if it allows pedagogy to take the lead some of the time – it will benefit as a discipline from a rebalancing in its own terms and a revival of interest and engagement. In schools, universities and public repute, theology has a 'nasty suspicion' about its looming redundancy, and is 'plagued by insecurity' about its language, meaning and relevance.[9] The disciplinary decline of theology is accentuated in the face of serious global threats – the pandemic, the climate crisis – which have further displaced theology from the intellectual centrality and control it once enjoyed. Influenced by a more fluid and equal relationship with the discipline of pedagogy, which is the prime discipline related to explanation and understanding, theology could find its renaissance, but only if power shifts.

Writing within a specific context, that of the Latin American Roman Catholic Church struggling between a vocation to serve the poor and an institutional tendency towards domination, Leonardo Boff astutely dissects the church's self-identity as *ecclesia discens* and *ecclesia docens* (a learning church and a teaching church).[10] Arguing that the entire church should be understood as learning and as teaching, he warns that 'if anyone in the church (Pope or bishops, especially) does not consider himself primarily as a member of the church *discens*, he ceases to be a sacramental member'.[11] The two functions have equal worth, apply equally to clergy and laity, and should be adjectives describing practices of the whole community of the church, rather than nouns referring to different divisions or sections of the institution.

Boff notes that there is a division of labour between learning and teaching in the church, and attributes this more to urbanization and the growth of hierarchies than to any specific will of Christ. He urges the church to engage in more analysis of the division of labour before making further distinctions between learning and teaching.[12] Extreme distinctions, in which the hierarchy does all the *docens* and the lay faithful do all the *discens*, are 'pathological', but he believes the church has the capacity to move towards a more healthy and valid relationship between learning and teaching within its own community.[13]

The imbalance between *discens* and *docens* is represented symbolically by the two stories in Chapter 2. We saw there that theology failed to engage in effective apologetics and was unable publicly to explain how to read a sacred text; it was unable, too, to accompany people on the learning journey towards deeper knowledge and understanding of the text. The church's specialists in theology – its clergy – could have benefited by referring to pedagogy. Pedagogy could have asked them: what are you trying to achieve? What is the knowledge you are trying to convey? What do you see as a successful reception of your message? What are the external factors you have to take into account, even though you cannot control them?

How do you intend to break down, structure and sequence the ideas in your message? Where do you want your hearers to go next with the new knowledge and understanding you have given them? If such questions had been asked of our two speakers in Chapter 2, perhaps they might have rewritten their presentations.

A related dimension in how theology is spoiled by its dominance and its neglect of pedagogy can be seen in preaching. When Karl Barth laid down a rule for the church that it should deliver its message in the way a postal worker delivers mail – 'the less it makes of it and the less it leaves on it its own fingerprints, the more it simply hands it on as it has received it ... so much the better',[14] he begged the question: what did the church receive, and how does the mere fact of living contextually change what we hear and share? Here, official theology has only partially accepted the lessons of its own sub-discipline, critical biblical scholarship, and has almost entirely rejected the lessons of its sister discipline, pedagogy.

The revolution in biblical scholarship is largely unknown to the church-going lay public. Original questions of historicity remain, but the tendency in preaching is to ignore them. Without that critical scrutiny, the text of a Gospel becomes 'as brittle as burned toast'.[15] The critical tools in the hands of academics can make for dry and awkward use, so that some adjustment is needed in order to apply critical theory in sermons or house groups.[16] But very little adjustment happens in parish churches. Unless we attend university churches or chapels, we might struggle to remember the last time we heard a sermon mentioning Gospel sources, redaction theory, authorial intent in the early church, or the Palestinian Jewish context. Even the acknowledgement that such critical tools exist, and can help in uncovering meaning in Scripture, is a rarity. This pedagogical deprivation probably has a negative effect on faith development. Invoking developmental psychology, Hull writes that 'religion can hold the believing adult in the stagnation of infancy or adolescence, but it can also become ... a rainbow bridge linking to various stages of ... life together'.[17] Again, pedagogy's intellectual habit of breaking the learning down, identifying the barriers to learning, and sequencing the steps of understanding, could be enormously salient to successful preaching. But again, this will only start to happen more widely if the power relationship shifts, and if theology starts to hold pedagogy in higher esteem.

A further illustration of the need to change the dance steps can be found in the contested subject of sexuality. It is now a widely accepted narrative that the decline in church attendance over the past 40 years has roots in the church's doctrinal statements and actions on priesthood and sexuality,[18] although this is not the whole explanation. Earlier in this chapter we saw how one teacher's educational convictions clashed with his church's position. The problem of sexuality can be broken down into pedagogical steps involving how the Bible is to be read and understood, and how pastoral contexts are to be interpreted, among others. The church's use of the Bible on matters of sexuality and gender has been criticized not only for biblicist literalism but also for the blunder of appealing to Scripture as a primary source when the conundrums of sexuality and gender are firstly a matter of practical ministry. In educational or pastoral work, reading the Scriptures is best done through the prism of the transformative love of Christ,[19] rather than attempting to define or delineate the love of Christ through the reading of bits of Scripture.

Similar hermeneutical weaknesses exist in those churches that have placed varying levels of prohibition on homosexuality. They have deployed a biblical hermeneutic of extracting ambiguous texts out of context and placing them into a late modern setting with the expectation that they will be taken as unambiguous and authoritative. This tactic has been viewed as inconsistent and anachronistic even within its own biblical terms.[20] Senior figures in the churches cannot agree among themselves on how the Bible is to be interpreted, or at what stage in the thinking it is best to refer to biblical sources. The pedagogical equivalent would be a group of science teachers teaching about an experiment, but disagreeing in front of the class about which equipment to use, how to conduct the test, and what the resultant findings are. Teachers know that the knowledge has to be clear, the method well tried, the sequence helpful; and where the information is contestable, that learners must be made aware of this at the right time, and shown the competent ways to observe the parameters of what is debatable. Nearly two centuries of evolutionary theory have left only a minor mark on theology as practised in churches and schools. It has become a minority view in Christian theology that the body of truth must evolve and work harder at understanding. Jack Mahoney, in his discussion of the church's troubled response to evolution, argues that theology must do more than develop; it must imitate evolution in order to behave as a living intellectual being and save itself from death. Two central concepts characteristic of evolutionary science, namely generosity and life, must be adopted as characteristics of theology. In this way, theology can become again the creative dialectic between belief and experience.[21]

Behind these conflicted examples stands the problem of theological education in the Christian church. Theological education and training for ministry are disabled by hermeneutical inconsistency, by the 'not in front of the children' posture in relation to critical readings of the Bible, and by failures of honesty on matters such as sexuality and evolution. Theological education occupies a conflicted zone between a process called 'education', which normally invokes clear rules of knowledge, discovery, change, insight and dynamism, and an inert body of official theological content called 'the truth', which will not change and can only be transmitted. Official theology therefore prefers to play only by educational rules in which the 'learner' is passive and absorbent.

Over the centuries, the power relationship has produced a poverty of theological understanding among Christian lay people, and a concomitant vulnerability. It has made Christians nervous in understanding Jesus, and hesitant to explore why it is difficult to understand him. It has made some of them afraid of theology. Knowing Jesus personally, loving him, believing in him and following him are all strong themes in the discourse of Christian discipleship and commitment; but understanding the truth claims made about him is a distinctly lower priority, and indeed is sometimes seen as undesirable and taboo. The churches generally lack a clear strategy for promoting an understanding of the one they call Lord, Teacher and Light of the world.

By comparison, the disciplinary capacity of pedagogy to operate self-critically, and to influence the practice of the teaching world in ways that challenge assumptions in and about classrooms, is high. The ability to deconstruct expertise before reconstructing it in a different way, to re-evaluate evidence, to challenge the common-sense beliefs at large in classrooms, and to issue moral challenges to the leaders of the profession, is a hallmark of recent writing by Daisy Christodoulou and others.[22]

A better balanced dance would see children and lay adults as theologians, as learners who can and need to be active in constructing meaning in partnership with qualified theologians and theological traditions.[23] The fact that this project is so often unsuccessful and leads to a buried theological and spiritual life in adults is evidence of the failure of educational nerve in theology.[24] It does not yet trust its dance partner.

The new steps: examples of theology learning from pedagogy

David Ford, reflecting on his experiences in theological education and scriptural reasoning, suggests five lessons from the collaboration between the church and academic theology. These are advisory principles, based on his practice. They shed light on the question Barth did not answer: how theology accounts for the cultural and pedagogical wrapping delivered by the gospel postal worker. For Ford, relationships between church and academy, and between gospel and culture, need to be characterized by innovative institutional creativity, historical and contextual particularity, riskiness, wisdom-seeking, and a concept of the church that is oriented to the previous four characteristics.[25] Ford is particularly interesting on the risks that theology must take: he is clear that 'the institutional default mode will usually favour an apparently safe institution under church control; a theology that takes the cross and the leading of the holy spirit seriously may encourage less of a "safety first" approach'.[26] And on a church oriented to seeking wisdom, Ford adopts a tone markedly less absolute than Barth's, yet more challenging:

> If God's generosity shares wisdom, knowledge and understanding far beyond the boundaries of the visible church, then there are institutional consequences of this: the church needs to relate to those institutions that contribute to seeking wisdom, knowledge and understanding, and to be concerned both to learn from them and to contribute to them.[27]

In similar vein, the Catholic theologian Paul Murray suggests key principles for receptivity to wider culture: 'our traditions are limited as well as life-giving, wounded as well as grace-bearing: we need to show rather than hide our wounds, and to ask our others to minister to us'.[28]

Modern protestant theology also contains the seeds of openness. Wolfhart Pannenberg believes that 'the most important task of Christology is ... to present the reasons for the confession of Jesus' divinity'.[29] This task, apologetics, cannot be achieved by insisting on *a priori* positions about Jesus' divinity, his status as saviour, or even the existence of a God. Some apprehension of the doctrinal positions, as a possible endpoint to the initial encounter, is pertinent and, according to Pannenberg, necessary, but no longer the only permissible endpoint for discourse about Christ.

Conclusion

Jesus no longer belongs exclusively to Christianity. The official church theologies have to unlearn the notions that Jesus is theirs, that they possess the whole truth about him, that they understand him and know how to speak about him and to him. When the unlearning has begun, then they can reconstruct

Christology. The powerful Easter proclamation that Christ is risen from the tomb – 'he is not here'[30] – means that Christ has escaped the powers of death, oppression and stultification, and is set free from the theological structures that would bind him. The people in our time who are resistant to hearing about him from the church can and do explore him through other frames.

Pedagogy can be an indispensable partner in the struggle to learn new steps. The internal structures of theological and particularly Christological thought can be brought into the light; the self-inflicted handicaps in theological communication, discussed in Chapter 2, can fall away if pedagogy is permitted to take the lead. Pedagogy's questions – how are we breaking down the knowledge? What do we expect learners to do? – are at heart friendly towards theology, and need not challenge its truthful insights. If the dance flows between them, how much more attractive and persuasive it will be.

Notes

1 Robin Alexander, 2008, *Essays on Pedagogy*, London and New York: Routledge, p. 3.

2 Jerome Bruner, 1996, *The Culture of Education*, Cambridge, MA: Harvard University Press, pp. 44ff.

3 A. Devlin, 2012, 'No place for prejudice in our schools', *The Guardian*, London: Guardian Newspapers, Monday 30 April, p. 25.

4 Natalie Wigg-Stevenson, 2014, *Ethnographic Theology: An inquiry into the production of theological knowledge*, New York: Palgrave Macmillan, p. 3.

5 Ros Stuart-Buttle, 2019, 'Catholic teachers, theological literacy and engagement with biblical texts', in Michael T. Buchanan and Adrian-Mario Gell (eds), *Global Perspectives on Catholic Religious Education in Schools*, 2, New York: Springer, pp. 179–90.

6 Richard Pring, 2001, 'Education as a moral practice', in Richard Pring, 2005, *Philosophy of Education: Aims, theory, common sense and research*, London: Continuum, pp. 11–25.

7 Melissa Benn, 2011, *School Wars: The battle for Britain's education*, London: Verso.

8 Parker J. Palmer, 1993, *To Know as We are Known: Education as a spiritual journey*, San Francisco, CA: Harper, p. ix.

9 Craig Dykstra, 1999, *Growing in the Life of Faith: Education and Christian practices*, Louisville, KY: Geneva Press, p. 9.

10 Leonardo Boff, 1990, *Church: Charism and power*, New York: Crossroad, pp. 138–43.

11 Boff, 1990, p. 138.

12 Boff, 1990, p. 140.

13 Boff, 1990, pp. 142–3.

14 Karl Barth, 2003, *God Here and Now*, New York: Routledge, p. 49.

15 Paul Laffan, 2019, *The Fabricated Christ: Confronting what we know about Jesus and the Gospels*, Minneapolis, MN: Fortress Academic Press, p. 1.

16 Nick Page, 2019, *The Badly Behaved Bible: Thinking again about the story of Scripture*, London: Hodder and Stoughton.

17 John Hull, 1985, *What Prevents Christian Adults from Learning?*, London: SCM Press, p. 159.

18 Andrew Brown and Linda Woodhead, 2016, *That Was the Church That Was: How the Church of England lost the English people*, London: Bloomsbury.

19 Stephen C. Barton, 1996, 'Is the Bible good news for human sexuality?', in Adrian Thatcher and Elizabeth Stuart (eds), *Christian Perspectives on Sexuality and Gender*, Grand Rapids, MI: Eerdmans, pp. 4–13.

20 Andrew Sullivan, 1995, *Virtually Normal: An argument about homosexuality*, London: Picador, pp. 25–55.

21 J. Mahoney, *Christianity in Evolution*, Washington, DC: Georgetown University Press, p. 167.

22 David Didau, 2015, *What if Everything you Knew about Education was Wrong?* Carmarthen, Crown House Publishing; Daisy Christodoulou, 2014, *Seven Myths about Education*, Abingdon: Routledge; Michael Fullan, 2003, *The Moral Imperative of School Leadership*, London: Sage.

23 G. Buttner, 2010, 'Where do children get their theology from?', in A. Dillen and D. Pollefeyt (eds), *Children's Voices: Children's perspectives in ethics, theology and religious education*, Leuven, Paris and Walpole, MA: Uitgeverij Peeters, pp. 357–72.

24 E. Champagne, 2010, 'Children's inner voice: Exploring children's contribution to spirituality', in Dillen and Pollefeyt (eds), pp. 373–96.

25 David Ford, 2013, 'Church and academy: Working relationships and theological rationales', unpublished paper for the Society for the Study of Theology, pp. 5–7.

26 Ford, 2013, p. 6.

27 Ford, 2013, pp. 6–7.

28 Paul Murray, 2014, 'Receptive ecumenism and ecclesial learning:

Learning to be church together', unpublished paper for the establishment of the National Centre for Christian Education, Liverpool Hope University, p. 2.

29 Wolfhart Pannenberg, ET 1968, *Jesus – God and Man*, London: SCM Press, p. 34.

30 Matthew 28.6.

4

Getting to know him

Introduction

In order to get closer to understanding Jesus as a learning
teacher, we must use a range of tools at our disposal. There are
many possible places to start: symbolically, the lectern, pulpit,
classroom, textbook, or critical commentary. My symbolic
starting point is just outside the church door. In this chapter
I want to clear the ground, establishing what we can know
about Jesus' life as a teacher, where the limits of our knowledge lie, how we can know it, and how best to approach the
Gospels as a source of that knowledge.

Many people in the church think they know about Jesus. If
we have been raised as Christians, or if we have been taught
about Christianity in school RE, there will be certain pieces of
information that we carry around. For Christians, Jesus looms
large in our personal devotions and the communal life of the
church. He has taken on a personality that is shaped in outline
by our own desire for him and coloured in by what we know
from worship, hymns, readings, sermons, and group work –
and equally shaped by what we do not know. He might be
'gentle Jesus meek and mild'; he might be the fierce prophet
of justice and righteousness; he might be a profound and
complex source of compassion and wisdom; he might be our
gracious friend; he might be our suffering saviour. Jesus has a
thousand faces in the imagination. The closer we come to him
the more we glimpse detail; but the less certain we can be that
our Jesus corresponds to anyone else's, or to reality. This is
potentially dangerous: 'perhaps the most deadening aspect of

our Christianity', warns the theologian Cynthia Bourgeault, is that 'we know the story. We know how the plot comes out. We know who the winners are, what the winning team is all about ... All this knowing about Jesus actually gets in the way.'[1] And Ann Christie warns of a spiritual 'routinization'[2] by which believers come to feel that the gospel has lost its tension.

To make headway in this enquiry we will move quite quickly over ground that has been broken by a century or more of scholars using critical literary tools to understand the text of the Gospels. The lessons from the critical tradition are crucial: that the Gospels do not provide a fully coherent narrative of Jesus' life and ministry; that nevertheless, certain strands of his life can be identified and relied on as the truthful experience of the communities that formed the text of the Gospels; that all the Gospels are written as post-resurrection material, selecting from oral stories to make sense of Jesus' purposes in the minds of those who already believed in him as the risen Lord. These are taken as the starting point of our enquiry.

How we read matters to what we read

If we read the Gospels flat on, as if they were direct records, we risk deceiving ourselves, and we miss much of the subtlety of their content. The Gospels are for the most part not a precise historical record: they are documents of the early church, mediating Christ to the wider church through memory, ritual and personal devotion, 'a picture of ... a picture'.[3] The fact that their mediation was itself a product of their context need not subtract from the revelatory nature of the Gospels, and can actually enhance it: many churches teach that those authors 'selected certain of the many elements which had been handed on, either orally or already in written form, others they synthesized or explained with an eye to the situation of the churches ... but always in such a fashion that they have told us the honest truth about Jesus'.[4]

Even so, literalist readings of the Gospels are still in wide circulation. Some theological traditions encourage this kind of reading, tending to steer round a critical historical approach,[5] perhaps in the belief that scholarship is too complicated or not open enough to discovering the real Jesus. In attempting to understand the context of Jesus' life, Gerd Theissen's light-hearted detective novel *The Shadow of the Galilean*,[6] which he wrote in the full knowledge that his colleagues might see it as a less than scholarly effort, is very useful in describing critically the historical circumstances as far as we can know them, and in getting under the skin of the Gospel narrative.

Lawrence Freeman provides us with a way of understanding how the literature we call the Gospels was formed:

> We can never know for sure, 'in fact', who wrote the Gospels attributed to Matthew, Mark, Luke and John. As texts they grew within both oral and written traditions but were further refined by personal prayer and communal discussion. People walked from place to place thinking of the stories and sayings that later coalesced in the texts we know. As in the first moments after the Big Bang, the bits and pieces of the cosmos of the Gospel were still in a disconnected and chaotic state in the early days of the Christian movement. By being told and retold they fell into shape and eventually into the form of the written texts we know. Each textual problem illustrates how a text represents the mind of a whole community for whom the individual is a channel.[7]

Since the emergence in Enlightenment Europe of a critical approach to reading the Bible, there has been a realization that the biblical material, composed of different genres, can be deceptive as well as revelatory. The tradition of scholarly search for the historical Jesus – the quest for a hard base of evidence about who he was and what he did – has been exhaustive, from Albert Schweitzer to Pope Benedict XVI.[8] The quest for the historical Jesus was a quintessentially modernist project aimed at establishing clear objective certainty.

Reception theory is the name given to the acknowledgement from the scholarly community that a definitive, authoritative and certain record of the historical Jesus is never going to be possible. But it is also an acknowledgement of the extensive influence of postmodern literary theory, that no text has a single meaning, and that meaning is not inherent in a text but is created by interaction between text and reader. The implication of this is that no single authoritative reading of the biblical text is permissible: instead, we see 'a coat of many postmodern colours, sheltering structuralists, Derridean deconstructionists' and others, all committed to seeing the text as 'a formalist enclosure'[9] in which no text's meaning is quite what it seems at first sight. The attempt to recover *the* original meaning of the Gospels is abandoned.

Even so, reception theory does not usually mean that 'anything goes' in the interpretation of the Bible. The temptation to surrender any clear knowledge about Jesus, collapsing into a helpless morass of mutual subjectivities, may be very great, particularly for lay Christian adults deprived of the critical tools for reading the text. This is something that can happen all too easily in small groups such as home-based Bible studies. In the face of this danger of subjectivity as a flight from doctrinal certainty, perhaps there is a need for a combination of letting go and holding on: letting go of doctrinal positions about him, because 'perhaps after all ... it does not matter a great deal what we say we believe about Jesus. How we judge him is less important than how he loves us';[10] and holding on to the profound challenge that he poses, which 'has a perennial power to open the eye of the heart and restore us to the true self',[11] and requires some theological understanding.

It is still necessary and permissible to identify a minimum of objective realities about the historical Jesus which all can agree as certain or probable by organizing the various ways in which the Gospel material has been received and interpreted, and giving them a meaningful narrative within their different historical contexts.

If we seek to know and understand Jesus as teacher, we have the refracted memory of his teaching as given to us, in various contexts, by his learners at a distance of 20 to 40 years. While some theologians claim that we can go back behind the texts 'to Jesus himself',[12] most scholars recognize that we cannot hope to penetrate beyond the Gospel texts. Rather than treating this reality as a hermeneutical barrier, we can accept it and take bearings from it.

What can we know about Jesus?

Several theologians have attempted to review what can be safely claimed about the historical Jesus. Geza Vermes's work, as he admits, is still a portrait rather than a photograph.[13] The Jesus who emerges from Vermes's study was a wise and remarkable man, a performer of astonishing deeds, a teacher of repentance and the kingdom of heaven, a man with a radical faith in God.

But it is of equal interest to identify what Jesus was not – or, more precisely, what we cannot assume about him from the reliable historical evidence:

- Not a speculative theologian; instead, he was interested solely in a this-worldly kingdom as a new reality, and believed that 'God is what God does'.[14]
- Not formally educated or qualified as a rabbi, but (perhaps because of this) filled with intensity, insight and power, highly literate in the Scriptures, speaking with immediacy, and following his unhesitating teacherly instincts of compassion towards outcasts and children.
- Not a first-century multiculturalist or universalist: he had little or no interest in Gentiles and no knowledge of wider religious cultures beyond his own.
- Not a gentle teacher: his eschatology (that is, his preaching of an imminent inbreaking of the kingdom of God into the realities of human history and society) was 'feverish'[15] at times, and his utterances were highly dramatic: You are wrong! Come out! Leave him! You hypocrites! You fools!
- Not a child prodigy: Vermes discounts any sense that Jesus might have had a back story of wondrous childhood achievements, and considers the genealogy linking him to David to have been a retrospective device. The absence of a back story heightens the drama of Jesus' appearance in Galilee,

particularly in Mark, where Jesus 'turns up suddenly like the hero of a novel or film'.[16]

- Finally, not the Christ of later doctrine, as developed and taught by the church. While the Gospels can be read so that they possess the roots of these doctrines, for Vermes they are 'definitely connected, yet ... also radically different'.[17] Paul's salvation theology, the Trinity, the insights of Christian philosophy, and the hierarchical church may or may not be faithful developments of the Gospel evidence, but they are developments, and do not fall within the realm of certainty based on Gospel evidence.

Of the many titles used for Jesus in the New Testament, that of 'Teacher' is used about 50 times, significantly more often than titles such as 'Son of David'; but Teacher is used very much less frequently than Son of Man, Christ, Lord or King.[18] He is described as teaching on countless occasions. It is, therefore, an important key to his identity, perhaps more in terms of what he *did* than *who he was*.

What seems clear is that Jesus was a Jewish teacher and preacher of wisdom, and of the inbreaking kingdom of God, and a specialist in apocalyptic preaching (the uncovering of divine mysteries). He understood the kingdom as a structural social and economic reality, characterized by spiritual, social and economic ways of living, not principally a legal matter.[19] The kingdom of God and its advance was his central interest.[20]

Jesus' teaching techniques consisted of rabbinical methods such as similes, epigrams, paradoxes, hyperboles, humour, questioning and disputation.[21] While teaching was central to Jesus' identity and dominant in the ways people addressed him, including his fellow rabbis, his teaching aims and messages were not always clear, which might lead us to question his effectiveness as a teacher.[22] However, it is widely accepted from the Gospels that:

- Jesus taught widely in large crowds, small groups and individuals, using words and signs.

- He used colourful stories and epigrams to convey an urgent message about the imminent kingdom of God.
- He taught in Aramaic and was a master of language, using it to contrast opposites, to create laughter, to quicken thought, to force moral choices, to reveal wisdom; he was both well versed in Hebrew Scripture and possessed of 'an original mind and a bold imagination'.[23]
- He narrated stories rooted in economic, social and emotional reality, and used them to provoke realization, as many other apocalyptic prophets had done before him.
- He saw children and the uneducated as models of receptivity and humility, and pointed to outcasts as first to understand and inherit the kingdom of God.
- He had unorthodox views on leadership, and frequently crossed swords with those in positions of authority.
- He was single-minded, passionate, and occasionally sharp-tongued.

In all, the portrait presents Jesus as a remarkable and unusual teacher, notwithstanding the questions about his teaching raised in Chapter 1.

Text and context

The layers that separate us from the original Jesus can be itemized as:

- The multilayered nature of the Gospel text, formed by the primitive Christian communities after the resurrection, taking oral material and memory, and placing it in forms and sequences that fitted with their contexts.
- The situatedness of Jesus and his followers in Israel, in the factional state of Judaism, with its divergent beliefs about itself, about God, about its Scriptures, and about its temple and authority structure; and how the factions in Israel interpreted their context, how they responded to diversity within Israel and to the political realities of Roman imperial power.

- The Christian church's development of doctrine on Christ, the Trinity and the Christian life over the 300 years after his death, followed by Christianity's gradual movement from persecuted minority to established religion; and how this affected its understanding of concepts such as the kingdom, including the history of the church's interaction with culture – rulers, armies, lawyers, merchants, revolutionaries, feminists – down to the present.
- Our own contexts in the nations, classes, communities, identities and families where we are.

To reach a literate, non-magical reading of the Gospels, these layers must be acknowledged. They may be seen as semipermeable membranes, either blocking or allowing our access to the authentic Christ; or as doors of perception – contexts in which our reflection can yield new insights.

Lasagne is a delicious Italian dish made of layers of flat pasta separated by a meat filling. The meat is not all at the bottom of the dish; it can be found at each level. We may sometimes assume that to reach the authentic Jesus we must burrow through successive layers of editorial and historical interpolation, the salvific equivalent of carbohydrate, before we can reach the pure salvific protein. But another way of understanding the Gospels is to see each layer as a source of nutrition, of insight, in itself. The intermediate layers in the Gospels and in the tradition need not be seen as obstacles, but as sources of revelation in their own way, speaking to each other and to the individual and communal Christian heart.

The social worlds of the Gospel editors

The editing role of the Gospel writers, with their influence in arranging and perhaps composing the orally remembered material into something with narrative flow, has massive implications for the church's reading of the Gospels – implications that, as we have seen in Chapter 2, rarely receive an adequate mention in preaching or teaching. To look at Jesus as a teacher, it helps if we recognize how each individual piece of oral memory about Jesus became a piece of text with a single concept, one or more verses in length (a *pericope*), that editors then placed in sequences that made sense to them in their different communities.

We know enough about the communities and contexts of the canonical Gospel writers to be able to discern their distinctive editorial hand. Of the four, probably two knew Jesus directly (Matthew and John); the other two were followers who had never met him but heard of him through leading apostles (Mark through Peter, and Luke through Paul). Mark's Gospel is the briefest and usually believed to be the earliest. It was probably composed for a community of Christians in Rome. In style, Mark is a pile-on of events, vividly and naively constructed, with limited theological reflection and little reference to Jewish Scripture. One feature is Mark's repeated mention of the disciples' lack of understanding of Jesus' teaching, of the kingdom, and of Messiahship.

Matthew, also known as Levi the former tax collector, was the main source and perhaps the direct author of the Gospel that bears his name. His is a Gospel for Jewish Christians in Palestine, particularly Galilee and Jerusalem. Matthew has a strong interest in Jesus' sayings and teachings, making him a source of particular importance for educators. He presents Jesus as the new Moses, the giver of the new law, and divides Jesus' discourses into five sections, echoing the five books of the Torah. To Matthew we owe the stylistic form of Jesus' epigrams. Because of his situation within a Christian community still entangled with Palestinian Judaism, Matthew has a particular interest in the boundaries that separate Christian from Jew, friend from enemy, pure from impure – a debate about church life that was topical and urgent at the time he was writing.

Linguistically, Luke is the most sophisticated Gospel, with a frame of reference to ideas and places beyond Judaism. This is not surprising when we note that Luke was also the author of Acts, he travelled with Paul and Barnabas, and spread the message to the Gentiles in Syria, Greece and perhaps Rome.

Luke is less interested in Jesus as the fulfilment of Jewish Scripture and more focused on him as a prophet and saviour in his own right. He noted that Jesus had a particular care for the marginalized, and drew admiration for his teaching.

In Part 2 of this book, Chapters 5 to 10 draw mainly from the three synoptic Gospels. Chapter 11 discusses the specific context and memory of John's Gospel. The role of the social and theological worlds inhabited by the authors is crucial in explaining the variations between the four Gospels, and also the way each of them is constructed:

> The Gospels are documents deeply impregnated with the beliefs of their producers, not the least of which was that the Messiah would fulfil prophecy. Jesus's life was not carefully stage-managed by him to have the appearance of doing that. It was made to look like it did in order to support the beliefs of his followers.[24]

Applying this methodological rule to a specific *pericope* of teaching, Laffan asserts:

> If Jesus is shown arguing with the Sadducees about the resurrection, this was not because such an argument had really occurred, it was because the reality of resurrection was a point of contention between the Sadducees and the early Christians. Mark 12:18–27 grew out of how the early Christians required a narrative in which their position was decisively vindicated against the Sadducees by Jesus's words.[25]

The ultimate destination of this reasoning was articulated in a sort of interpretive rule of thumb that Jesus' Messiahship began with the resurrection and was projected back into the material on his preaching and teaching.[26] It is likely that much else in the Jesus-memory began with the resurrection experience, and was then retrospectively inserted, and we shall see examples of this in Part 2.

Borrowing from Emile Durkheim and adapting a sociological notion of religion as a product of society, the biblical scholar

Philip Esler contends that Luke-Acts, Matthew and John were all written for specific 'social worlds',[27] which were concrete Christian communities or ensembles of communities with distinctive social structures – and that the social world influenced the development of the most primitive or early version of the Christian proclamation (the *kerygma*). Thus, the fragmented Jewish context of those early communities, and the larger contact with Gnostic and Greek thought experienced by the Johannine community, created a setting in which the memory started to form solidly. The *kerygma* can be seen as a stem cell from which the credal body was grown. At its heart, in one of its earliest forms as expressed by Peter in his Pentecost address (long before the Gospels were written down), it proclaimed this:

> Jesus the Nazarene was a man commended to you by God by the miracles and portents and signs that God worked through him when he was among you ... This man, who was put into your power by the deliberate intention and foreknowledge of God, you took and had crucified ... You killed him, but God raised him to life ...[28]

In highly condensed and dramatic form, everything that later became the story of the Gospels – prophecies and divine promises fulfilled, healing, conflict, death, resurrection – is there in Peter's speech: everything, that is, except teaching. It is strange that Jesus the teacher has no mention in this earliest form of the Christian message; an omission that has been repeated in theological method many times since.

What did Jesus teach?

Most of this book is an enquiry into the *nature* of Jesus as a teacher, and the relationship between his teaching and his identity as the Christ. This necessarily sets aside an extensive discussion of the *content* of his teaching, important though that question is. But having explored the limits of what can be certainly known about Jesus in his context, we can briefly attempt a summary of his main teaching messages. Jesus, it seems, began as a follower of John the Baptist, who was later arrested and executed; and Jesus ended up on the cross. Between those two events, he spent a period of perhaps two or three years teaching and preaching. He taught a golden rule of reciprocal ethics, which appears frequently in religions and philosophies; he also taught specific ethical and spiritual requirements of a coming kingdom in which normal values would be reversed. He has been summarized as 'a philosopher ... [of] the golden rule ... a peasant poet who has enriched Jewish literature with marvellous stories ... a unique prophet'.[29]

We may find it hard to categorize Jesus as a teacher of any particular subject. It does not help much to think of him as a teacher of religion, as if religion were separable from any other aspects of life. Among the things that Jesus did teach about were ethics, Jewish Scripture (the law and the prophets particularly), how to interpret Scripture (hermeneutics), and the coming kingdom of God. Arguably, he taught simply about God.

According to Vermes,[30] Jesus preached a coming kingdom, and preached it exclusively to Jews. The kingdom was imminent, and Jesus believed it would be realized during his lifetime and as a result of his teaching.[31] His title Son of Man refers to the apocalyptic vein in Jewish Scripture. Jesus probably did not expect his teaching career to be terminated with violent death. He taught an absolute trust in God, the importance of prayer, the need to become like children, an eschatological concept of family, healing and exorcism as signs of the imminent kingdom, and ethical behaviour summarized in a series of hyperbolic verbal tricks. The radical nature of his message is commonly acknowledged:

> The God who is coming is altogether different from the one that man expects ... Religiously initiated and educated man is completely deceived ... God's revelation destroys every picture which man's desires make of it ...[32]

Revelation, tradition and myth

We can have access to a degree of clarity about who Jesus was, and what he taught, as long as we avoid the temptation to turn a degree of clarity into an idol of certainty. At its best, the Christian tradition helps us to avoid that danger by holding together a number of divergent images of Jesus and inviting us to use the tools of textual criticism and interpretation. The use we make of these tools is a process, rather than a once-for-all task.

The theologian David Heywood's study of the interface between divine revelation and human learning argues that God's revealing of self works with reason, history, and the natural development of ideas over time, rather than overriding them. The 'definitive truth' of revelation, which can 'only be arrived at conceptually by a process', nevertheless depends upon God breaking into the circle of human thought with a new hermeneutic that serves as a 'foundation for understanding both ourselves and the world'.[33]

Christ himself has to make a journey from his culture to ours. This journey is not magical, and his words and deeds are not instantly transferable. His encounter with us relies on a degree of understanding about his context, as well as the work of the spirit. Heywood strikes a balance:

The incarnate Christ ... is ... to be understood as a figure of history ... His actions and teaching can only be correctly understood in the context of his own culture ... At the same time, Jesus is a super-historical figure [whose challenge] concerns not simply the identity of Jesus but of oneself as well ... While Christian faith rests on the historical reality of Jesus's life, death and resurrection, his truth can only be discovered in personal encounter.[34]

Heywood underscores the importance of a process of dynamic relationship between revelation and learning when he asserts that 'revelation is a learning process, which uses all the natural processes of human learning, but in which the subject is God himself through Jesus Christ and in which the dynamism of the Holy Spirit is added to the natural agency of the human individual'.[35]

We saw in Chapter 2 how the long pilgrimage from childlike faith to something more complex can feel so perilous that even experienced preachers and teachers are afraid to send young people on the journey. Misunderstandings of revelation, truth, myth and tradition are likely. There is no short cut to a place of hermeneutic safety and simplicity. In the Gospel accounts of Jesus' life and death we have 'a unique combination of history and myth'.[36] Our task is to understand it.

The mythological material in the Gospels need not be an obstacle to understanding their core message; but the theologian's task is to identify history and myth, separating them out yet also noting how they blend; to enable others to understand the text, and allow the word of God to speak; 'to make the Gospel comprehensible as a call addressed to us'.[37]

Notes

1 Cynthia Bourgeault, 2008, *The Wisdom of Jesus: Transforming heart and mind*, Boston, MA: pp. 2–3.

2 Ann Christie, 2012, *Ordinary Christology*, Burlington, VT and Farnham: Ashgate, p. 179.

3 Jaroslav Pelikan, 1985, *Jesus through the Centuries: His place in the history of culture*, New Haven, CT: Yale University Press, p. 10.

4 Austin Flannery (ed.), 1975, '*Dei Verbum*: Dogmatic Constitution on Divine Revelation', in *Vatican Council II*, Dublin: Dominican Publications, pp. 750–65, p. 761.

5 Tom Wright, 2011, *Simply Jesus: Who he was, what he did, why it matters*, New York: HarperCollins.

6 Gerd Theissen, ET 1987, *The Shadow of the Galilean*, London: SCM Press.

7 Lawrence Freeman, 2000, *Jesus: The teacher within*, NY and London: Continuum, p. 72.

8 Edgar V. McKnight, 2009, *Jesus Christ Today: The historical shaping of Jesus for the twenty-first century*, Macon, GA: Mercer.

9 M. Lieb, E. Mason and J. Roberts (eds), 2011, *The Oxford Handbook of the Reception History of the Bible*, Oxford: Oxford University Press.

10 Freeman, 2000, p. 264.

11 Freeman, 2000, p. 264.

12 Wolfhart Pannenberg, ET 1968, *Jesus – God and Man*, London: SCM Press, p. 24.

13 Geza Vermes, 2003, *The Authentic Gospel of Jesus*, London: Allen Lane.

14 Vermes, 2003, p. 412.

15 Vermes, 2003, p. 408.

16 Vermes, 2003, p. 398.

17 Vermes, 2003, p. 414.

18 Freeman, 2000, p. 40.

19 Brad Young, 1993, *Jesus the Jewish Theologian*, Ada, MI: Baker Academic.

20 Matthew 11.12.

21 Craig Evans, 2002, 'The misplaced Jesus: Interpreting Jesus in a Judaic context', in B. Chilton, C. Evans and J. Neusner, *The Missing Jesus: Rabbinic Judaism and the New Testament*, Leiden and Boston, MA: Brill, pp. 11–40, pp. 24–7.

22 Charles Melchert, 1998, *Wise Teaching: Biblical wisdom and educational ministry*, Harrisburg, PA: Trinity Press International, 1998, pp. 214–16.

23 Vermes, 2003, p. 395.

24 Paul Laffan, 2019, *The Fabricated Christ: Confronting what we know about Jesus and the Gospels*, Minneapolis, MN: Fortress Academic Press.

25 Laffan, 2019, p. 10.

26 William Wrede, 1971, *The Messianic Secret*, Cambridge: James Clark.

27 Philip Esler, 1994, *The First Christians in their Social Worlds: Social scientific approaches to New Testament interpretation*, London: Routledge, p. 6.

28 Acts 11.22–25.

29 Theissen, 1987, pp. 130–9.

30 Vermes, 2003, pp. 370–97.

31 Leander E. Keck, 2000, *Who is Jesus? History in perfect tense*, Columbia, SC: University of South Carolina Press, pp. 65ff.

32 Paul Minear, 1984, *Matthew, the Teacher's Gospel*, London: Darton, Longman and Todd, p. 146.

33 David Heywood, 2004, *Divine Revelation and Human Learning: A Christian theory of knowledge*, Aldershot: Ashgate, pp. 152, 158.

34 Heywood, 2004, pp. 156, 158.

35 Heywood, 2004, p. 168.

36 R. Bultmann, 1973, 'Kerygma and Myth', in E. Tinsley (ed.), *Modern Theology*, London: Epworth Press, pp. 137–46, p. 137.

37 R. Bultmann, 1973, p. 137.

PART 2

Learning teacher

There is much unrealized insight about Jesus the teacher as portrayed in the Gospels. By reflecting, as a teacher, on Jesus' teaching encounters – his parables, sayings, arguments, tricks of imagery and language – I hope to bring some half-buried gospel themes to the surface. The chapters in Part 2 explore the text of the Gospels with the aim of establishing what can be said about him as a teacher, and in what ways the text places limits to our insight.

When preparing this part of the book, I found that there were several ways to approach a study of the half-visible teacher in the Gospels. A study of each Gospel in turn would have succeeded in rehearsing the specific editorial interest of each source, but I concluded that as an approach it would miss what I was looking for – the half-buried evidence of the workings of Jesus' teaching mind. Instead, I began to try hearing a teacher's voice in the Gospels, listening for repeated turns of phrase that convey the characteristic ways in which a fellow teacher presents ideas. And those phrases came; they accrued meaning in their early church context. Some of the characteristic phrases of Jesus the teacher are now chapter headings in Part 2.

We begin at the resurrection. Virtually everything that the Gospels say about Jesus as teacher, Lord and Messiah originates from the experience of meeting him in his risen state. So Chapter 5 takes three resurrection experiences that involve teaching in three very different ways, and begins to build tentative yet revealing portraits of the teacher who feels, looks and sounds extraordinarily different each time, varying according to who is being taught. In Chapters 6 and 7, Jesus' interest in the Torah and the prophets – how to read and interpret them

– is examined, and we see both the similarity with rabbinical methods and the roots of his confrontation with the authorities. The geographical locations of his teaching, and the significance that temple, synagogue and wilderness have as metaphorical classroom settings, is the subject of Chapter 8. Central to the search for Jesus the teacher is the problem of his obscurity, the way in which he seems sometimes to hide his meaning from learners, setting them up to fail and then condemning them for failing. It is a significant fault line in his image. Chapter 9 examines this faultline through the context of Matthew's Gospel, and asks whether Jesus was after all a good teacher. A small and much overlooked crisis in Jesus' teaching, which could have been a pivotal moment in joining his teaching mission to his death, is explored through his question, 'How shall we picture the kingdom?' in Chapter 10. Finally, in Chapter 11 John's Gospel is treated as a theologically rich memory of a beloved teacher. John's remembrance is of a teacher and Lord who through many twists and turns – somewhat akin to the learning journey feared by many in today's church – draws his learners to himself. The memory is simultaneously personal and universal in its scope.

Jesus the teacher has many faces in these seven studies. I cannot say that a coherent, homogenized teacher emerges. It would be surprising if he did, given the very distinctive contexts of the four writers and their role in editing the oral memories of their communities. Even so, a learning teacher emerges – a Jesus who could not possibly be described as programmatic or predestined, a teacher who made mistakes and risked everything for the sake of the kingdom. As we walk through the synoptic Gospels in Chapters 6 to 10, we track his teaching ministry from his passionate love of the Torah and expectation of the kingdom, through the early clashes over his authority and on towards the temple confrontation. We may begin to discern some unifying themes. His path to glorification was strewn with pedagogical boulders, the fallen rocks of his culture and his own assumptions, blocking his way and acting as barriers to understanding for his hearers. The full humanity of his teacherliness becomes, I hope, a little more visible through these chapters. So, I hope, does his full divinity – but do not let us rush ahead to the empty tomb. To understand how he taught, we need to detect the pedagogical path he could have trodden, and walk it ourselves.

5

The other side of you: The risen Christ as trickster teacher

Introduction

In view of the resurrection prism through which the Gospels are composed, it seems appropriate to begin our search for Jesus the teacher from 'the other side', in the post-resurrection narratives, where we find the most fresh, emotionally charged, complex and revealing dialogues – encounters that create the theological meaning of much that is narrated leading up to them. Three narratives that can shed particular light on Jesus the teacher are his conversation with Thomas, his encounter with two disciples on the way to Emmaus, and his appearance in the garden to Mary Magdalene. They are treated here in that order, an ascending order of textual, Christological and pedagogical complexity.

Give me your hand: Jesus teaches Thomas

Thomas stands out as the disciple who had not been present when Jesus appeared to the other ten, showing them his wounds.[1] We rarely pause to wonder why this was so – the reason may have been unimportant – but his absence creates a distance between his cognitive state and that of his fellows. Thomas needs to know: he appears to be the type of person who requires objective data before being able to make any meaningful response. We have seen him expressing this cognitive need before in relation to Jesus and where he is going.[2] When Thomas is told of the appearance of the risen Jesus, his unbelief is expressed in a specific way that suggests an interesting cognitive position: Thomas wants to see and touch Jesus' wounds. It almost seems as if his cognitive blockage is to do with the crucifixion, rather than the resurrection. Or perhaps he will only believe if he can establish some kind of cause and effect: that the risen apparition is the same man who had been executed. And so the scene is set for an epistemological denouement in which everyone else's joy in the resurrection is tested by establishing beyond doubt that the tragedy had happened, and happened to the same man. A week later, this is what unfolds. 'The doors were closed, but Jesus came in and stood among them.'[3] We may or may not interpret this entry into the room as miraculous; but the mention of closed doors (*thuron* are doors and also opportunities), repeating what had happened on the previous occasion, has a suggestion of a closed cognitive state into which Jesus is able to break.

With Thomas, Jesus is a compassionate and insightful teacher. Breaking gently into Thomas's mind, he appears to know the proof that Thomas needs, without being asked. Thomas as a learner is worth taking extra trouble over. Jesus, wishing them all peace, is peaceful and gentle with Thomas. There is no criticism or judgement. Thomas is invited to apply his test of physical touch to verify that this Jesus was the same one who had endured suffering. 'Give me your hand: put it into my side' is an invitation to cognitive collaboration and identification: feel what I feel, know what I know. Doubt no longer.

Perhaps – this is entirely speculative – Thomas had been absent previously because he was in doubt, and needed to be alone, processing the tragedy and the rumours of resurrection, weighing them all up in his mind. Now, taken by the hand and shown the clear knowledge understanding he craved, he voices his gratitude and joy.

Thomas, with his need to know all about, to inquire and verify, to substantiate and validate, provided the entire community of disciples with opportunity for faith informed with feeling, considered belief, and experience of the fullness of the message of Christ.[4]

Thomas may be, for us, one archetype of a learner. He meets and follows a risen Christ who recognizes what he needs, and brings him to fresh insight, and to life-changing realization, with a gentle touch.

The anonymous trickster of Emmaus

Luke's story of the appearance of Jesus to two disciples on the road to Emmaus[5] has struck many as a strange narrative. It contains some problems of plot, such as how Jesus fell in step with them; the failure of Cleopas and the other disciple to recognize their Lord even though they knew him (they were not of the eleven, but were closely in touch with the inner circle of disciples); the undeclared identity of the other disciple; and the mysterious disappearance of Jesus at the moment of recognition. In Mark's brief parallel of the story, Jesus 'showed himself under another form'.[6] The Greek word for form, *morphe*, also suggests nature; the word for showing himself, *ephanerothe*, is from *phaino*, to appear or become visible, and carries connotations of apparition, revelation, and shining. The episode bears strong resemblance to a subsequent episode recorded by Luke in Acts: the encounter between Philip and the Ethiopian,[7] which has the same structure of journey, ignorance of Scripture, explanation, invitation, sacramental moment and sudden disappearance. Some common root, in the form of a quasi-mystical experience in the early Christian church, seems quite likely.

These puzzling plot features have prompted some commentators to see the story as mythological,[8] and others to treat it as a confused dream of longing (suggested, for example, by T. S. Eliot's reference in *The Waste Land*: 'But who is that on the other side of you?'[9]).

Others have focused on Luke's nice arrangement of the ironies in the plot structure: that the one about whom they are so passionately talking is with them, that they ask him if he is the only one who has not heard about Jesus, and that he himself fills in the gaps in their understanding.[10] Throughout the encounter on the road and at the meal, the word 'Lord' (*Kyrios*) is not used once, despite its being so central to Luke's overall portrait of Christ, 'the heart of the Lukan message'.[11] It is only used when the two rush back to Jerusalem. Jesus' Lordship in this story is disguised: Jesus remains a half-hidden, ambiguous figure, speaking of himself in the third person, explaining the Scriptures concerning himself and repeating his own actions at the last supper. Not for the first time in the Gospels, a dramatic irony brings the reader close to the writer in a way that excludes the principal characters: we are told it is Jesus, but they do not know; Jesus knows they do not know, and Luke knows that we do know. We are invited to agree with Jesus' judgement that the disciples are foolish or stupid (*anoetos*, a word used in Greek comedy[12]) and slow of heart. We are permitted a certain superior smile at the disciples' blunder and a sympathy with Jesus' patient and lengthy explanation of the necessity of his own suffering.

Conscious that the post-resurrection encounters set the scene for all that precedes them, we might find the road to Emmaus inauspicious as a foundation for a good pupil–teacher dynamic. Jesus the teacher seems here to be a trickster: his appearances and disappearances are rather random, his riddling approach feels edged with slight teasing. Luke's irony makes us complicit with a teacher who metaphorically rolls his eyes at us in mock despair over his disciples' inability to understand; his pedagogical approach to them seems a little unloving, his expectations of them unfairly high. Yet it is possible to detect a dialectic between Cleopas and his teacher, with Cleopas supplying what he knows of the story, at which point the teacher completes it with meaning, revealing the divine necessity of the cross and the meaning of the Scriptures. Jesus the teacher uses questions to solicit the story and to provoke deeper understanding. A second look at the structure of the conversation does suggest a certain sympathetic connection between teacher and disciples.

The manner of his teaching in this resurrection encounter is of importance and is unfolded slowly by Luke in the knowledge that it will be recognized by Christian readers. Jesus teaches them the meaning of their experience in three ways that are master metaphors of learning: the journey, the explanation and the sacramental meal.[13] By turns, his walking with them is symbolic of a teacher's care and identification with his learners; his use of words, questioning and explanation are part of any teacher's stock-in-trade; and his action in breaking bread – Luke's choice of words here being similar enough to his account of the last supper[14] to allow any reader to see the connection – establishes the emotional connection of communion that underpins the teaching function of the church's liturgy. Underneath the events of the story – walk, talk, meal – there lies a teacher's intention first to identify with learners and win their trust, next to inform them systematically through questioning, dialogue and exposition, and finally to deepen the intensity of their learning, and their long-term memory, through ritual.

That this strategy strikes home successfully is seen in the disciples' comment after he has left them: 'Did not our hearts burn within us …?'[15] From this it is clear that an insight into successful teaching exists in the post-resurrection community's earliest experiences of Jesus: Luke's Jesus is a teacher who knows and practises the importance of emotional connection and knowledgeable explanation in leading to understanding. The risen Christ is experienced by his followers and believers as a rare teacher: challenging, perhaps even sharp-tongued, but systematic, intriguing and bound to them through sacrament.

Do not touch me: knowledge lost and found

John's account of the meeting between Mary Magdalene and the risen Jesus[16] is similarly mystifying, although it takes place in a different emotional key. The encounter is unique to John's Gospel, although elements of it appear in the non-canonical Gospel of Mary and other apocryphal fragments. Like the walk to Emmaus, it features some plot puzzles, includes the motif of the unrecognized stranger, and is charged with considerable emotional depth; but the dissimilarities weigh more: there is no playful irony, and the story has recurrent notes of closeness and distance, perhaps even a submerged eroticism. The 'most humanly moving of all the stories of the risen Christ',[17] it commands our attention because of the uniquely intense relationship of teacher and disciple at its heart.

There is an immediacy and physicality from the start, expressed through the present tense and through the pointers that Mary Magdalene comes looking for Jesus' body and weeps at the loss of it. His corpse has been anointed with aloes and myrrh, a combination that also occurs in the Song of Songs[18] where another woman is searching for her missing lover and questioning strangers as to where he might be.[19]

Mary Magdalene's single word of recognition, 'Rabbouni', is of central significance to our search for the risen Jesus as teacher, primarily because she does not call him 'Lord' at that point, even though she has spoken of him as Lord (Kyrios) twice in the moments before recognition. The Aramaic Rabbouni may be variously translated as 'my teacher', 'my dear teacher' or 'my God'.[20] The note of personal intimacy in the pronoun has a powerful and yet tantalizingly unclear hinterland in the apocryphal literature. A Manichean psalm book has Mary calling him 'Rabbi, my master' and Jesus replying with his own pet name for her: 'Marihamme, Marihamme, wipe the tears from your eyes and know me';[21] the Gospel of Mary is insistent in chapter 22.55–59 that Jesus loved her very well, and gives in chapter 9 a fragmentary resurrection encounter narrative, described as a vision, after which she says to the disciples, 'I have seen the Lord' – the same words as in John 20.18. The encounter may or may not be the same as that in the garden.[22] Yet John's own translation of Rabbouni is simply 'teacher' – perhaps a first indication that something is not being said, and that the full emotional freighting of the word is not being acknowledged. In public she calls him Lord; in private, a name that is deeply personal and unique; and he uses her name, something he does for no other woman in the fourth Gospel.[23] The

Gospel narrative 'zooms in on the teacher–disciple relationship at this moment of encounter and recognition'.[24]

Are we, then, able to look more into the nature of this recognition? The earlier part of the account gives the impression of Mary Magdalene as being confused. She goes off, then comes back without her companions. Jesus is not in disguise, yet even when he speaks to her she does not recognize him; that moment only comes when he uses her name. Whatever has blocked her cognition, be it grief or disbelief (there is no suggestion of stupidity, as there is with the Emmaus narrative), has suddenly and dramatically been removed. Larsen calls this moment 're-cognition',[25] a new ordering of knowledge: this and other recognition moments are 'exponents of a new situation'.[26] In describing Mary as 'turning towards' Jesus (*strapheisa*, from *strepho*, to turn around) at that moment, there is more than a hint that this was an inward change as much as it was an outward physical turning. As such it was also a mental and emotional turning.[27] Her new knowledge is personal: a unity of mind, heart and body.

What happens next in John's narrative creates a dissonance that has attracted much critical attention. Jesus' instruction, '*me mou haptou*',[28] has been speculatively translated as 'do not touch me', 'do not cling to me', 'do not keep clinging to me', 'do not cling to me now' or 'do not hold me back'. The phrase has 'an astonishing multiplicity of meanings'[29] and is by most accounts a difficult text. It seems to shatter the joyous intimacy of the previous sentence. The instruction does not appear in the Gospel of Mary. This may or may not mean that the Johannine church inserted the saying because of their concern to maintain the purity and asceticism of Jesus – and that in a passage that had already included several suggestions of the opposite. Yet the negation of intimacy is strong evidence that intimacy had existed; it is suggestive of Mary Magdalene's desire to continue, through physical touch, a friendship that had pertained until recently.

Whatever the exact nature of that relationship, which we cannot know, our task here is to understand the interchange in the context of disciple and teacher. Jesus' reason, 'for I have not yet ascended to the father', is of limited help. It seems to mean that the earthly reality of his physical presence, which she had lost and found, was about to be lost again. It might be a prelude to his next instruction, which is to go and teach, signalling an emotional change from dependent pupil to authorized apostle. It could be taken to mean that there is a form of knowledge of Jesus that is more deep than touching or embracing. Possibly it represents an early church view that close physical contact between the risen Lord and a woman was impure. We have already seen how, a week or more later, Thomas is permitted and encouraged to touch the risen Lord; so close physical contact seems to be proscribed only when it is between a man and a woman, or when it is charged with emotion.

Our interest in Jesus as teacher, and our observation of his command not to touch followed by his commission to Mary to teach and instruct, makes a case for an epistemological understanding of 'noli me tangere'. Their way of knowing each other, and their shared knowledge of God, is now on a different footing entirely: not less intimate, but transcending its former intimacy. Mary has stepped up to being Jesus' fellow teacher, and been given an authority to tell the others of the resurrection and shape their new identity. In this sense, what she is told not to cling to is her former understanding of him and of herself; this must change because he will soon be ascending to his father, and she must lead. This is filled out in the Gospel of Mary, where she teaches the male disciples, comforts them in their perplexity and fear, and turns their hearts to God.[30] In the apocryphal account, the chronology of her vision(s) and teaching is not very clear except that it is definitely post-resurrection; and her vision of Jesus is an intimate conversation on how one perceives God, through soul, spirit or mind.[31] This is consistent with an insight that the Johannine 'noli me tangere' signalled an epistemological change.

When we review the plot structure and compare it with the other two post-resurrection teaching encounters discussed here, does a systematic picture of the risen teacher emerge? If Thomas's teacher is one who gently breaks into the mind in order to take the learner by the hand, and if Luke's Emmaus story employs the master metaphors of journey, explanation and liturgical meal, then the corresponding choice of structure in John's garden story is of intimacy and personal knowledge gained, lost and gained again in a new form. Just as there is triumph in Jesus' broken body rising again, so also there is redemption in Mary Magdalene's knowledge – a physical and emotional knowledge – being broken and restored. The setting is a garden, reminiscent of that mythical garden in which humankind's knowledge was first corrupted. In this new garden, at the start of the week and early in the morning, we symbolically witness an epistemological resurrection: the inauguration of a new way of knowing, learning and teaching.

The risen Christ and epistemology

All these resurrection encounters have at their heart an interest in how we know, teach and learn. In all three, Jesus appears and disappears mysteriously in order to bring knowledge to very different people. The stories share an epistemological project – in Larsen's view, something they have in common with several classical and other Gospel narratives of encounters with strangers. Larsen theorizes that the disguised stranger is an authorial device for epistemological subversion:

When ... characters like the impostor, the trickster, the make-believer, the metamorph, the apparent stranger, the reflective observer, or the hero in disguise enter the stage, the plot inevitably becomes a masquerade where suspense centers on the cognitive play of semblance and truth.[32]

And yet, when the tension is released by the moment of recognition, we see that a believing acceptance had all along been the purpose of the narrative (as indicated, for example, in John's signing-off statement, 'these [signs] are recorded so that you may believe that Jesus is the Christ'.)[33] But belief is not like any other form of knowledge. The recognition moment always 'brings to the surface the question of the epistemological status of events and claims'.[34] Thomas's risen teacher is entirely gentle, while Luke's companion on the Emmaus road is a trickster, simultaneously mocking his disciples' confusion and systematically repairing it; and Mary's risen Rabbi is a metamorph, the subject of her deepest knowledge and desire, and perhaps of John's too, who transforms the rules of their relationship.

Whether or not we can reconcile these forms in one teacher is perhaps not the point. Perhaps he is a teacher of multiple personalities, known for surprising his pupils not only in the variety of his techniques but also in the playfulness with which his meanings and his methods appear, disappear and reappear. There are plentiful glimpses of this surprising teacher in the narratives that lead up to the passion, and it is to some of these that we now turn.

Notes

1 John 20.24–29.

2 John 14.5.

3 John 20.26.

4 Suzanne Zuercher, 1992, *Enneagram Spirituality: From compulsion to contemplation*, Notre Dame, IN: Ave Maria Press, p. 64.

5 Luke 24.13–35.

6 Mark 16.12–13.

7 Acts 8.26–40.

8 C. F. Evans, 1990, *Saint Luke*, London: SCM Press and Philadelphia, PA: Trinity Press International, p. 905.

9 T. S. Eliot, 1940, *The Waste Land*, London: Faber and Faber, lines 359–65, p. 41.

10 Evans, 1990, p. 886.

11 F. Bovon, 2006, *Luke the Theologian*, Waco, TX, Baylor University Press, p. 135.

12 Evans, 1990 p. 909.

13 F. Craddock, 1990, *Luke: A Bible commentary for teaching and preaching*, Louisville, KY: John Knox Press, pp. 285–6.

14 Luke 22.19.

15 Luke 24.32.

16 John 20.1–18.

17 C. H. Dodd, 1954, *The Interpretation of the Fourth Gospel*, Cambridge: Cambridge University Press, p. 441.

18 John 19.39; Song of Songs 4.14.

19 R. Goss, 2006, 'John', in D. Guest, R. Goss, M. West and T. Bohache (eds), *The Queer Bible Commentary*, London: SCM Press, pp. 548–65; and D. Carr, 2003, *The Erotic World: Sexuality, spirituality, and the Bible*, New York: Oxford University Press, pp. 164–7.

20 R. E. Brown, 1971, *The Gospel According to John*, London: Chapman, pp. 991–2.

21 E. Mohri, 2013, '*Noli Me Tangere* and the Apocrypha', in R. Bieringer, K. Demasure and B. Baert (eds), *To Touch or Not to Touch? Interdisciplinary perspectives on the Noli Me Tangere*, Leuven: Peeters, pp. 83–98, p. 87.

22 C. Tuckett, 2007, *The Gospel of Mary*, Oxford: Oxford University Press, pp. 169ff.

23 E. de Boer, 2004, *The Gospel of Mary: Listening to the beloved disciple*, London and New York: Continuum, p. 161.

24 Mohri, 2013, p. 79.

25 K. B. Larsen, 2008, *Recognizing the Stranger: Recognition scenes in the Gospel of John*, Leiden and Boston, MA: Brill, p. 222.

26 Larsen, 2008, p. 222.

27 Larsen, 2008, p. 202.

28 John 20.17.

29 R. Bieringer, 2013, 'Touching Jesus?', in Bieringer, Demasure and Baert (eds), pp. 61–81, p. 68.

30 Alan Jacobs, 2016, *The Gnostic Gospels*, London: Watkins, pp. 53–62.

31 Tuckett, 2007, p. 171.

32 Larsen, 2008, p. 25.

33 John 20.31.

34 Larsen, 2008, p. 32.

6

Go and learn the meaning of the words: The roots and formation of a teacher

The Torah

It all began with the Torah. His knowledge of it, his love of it, and his growing capacity to get inside it – to discern its spirit as deeply as he knew its letters. As described by Matthew, Jesus is an energetic teacher, an arguer, not unlike the scribes or Pharisees. Some have suggested that this was also Matthew's identity, if any individual of that name existed.[1] Jesus, on his return to Nazareth, astounded the synagogue with his knowledge of the Torah, and with something else – a wisdom and power they were unaccustomed to, and which they had trouble reconciling with the fact that he was a local.[2]

In the account of his preaching at Nazareth, there is a hint that he had been away and come back, and the difference in him is somehow attributed to his time away. Teachers often ask each other, 'Where did you train?' – it is a useful conversation opener, and quite often a short cut to understanding the colleague's pedagogical perspective on their profession and subject. Where did Jesus' knowledge and wisdom come from? Where did he 'train', who were his masters, what did he bring back? A ready answer is that it was all given to him from God, the one he called his father – too easy an answer, if we take seriously his full humanity, participating in the normal cognitive processes of thought and development, as any teacher does. For educational insights into the roots of Jesus' rabbinical knowledge, we must also eschew the attractive notion that he was a charismatically inspired, non-literate peasant-prophet.[3] His utterances are prophetic and original, but they are also highly literate, steeped in a knowledge and understanding of Scripture – a knowledge that must have come from somewhere in the rainbow of Israel's religious life. But Jesus has no absolute adherence to any particular strand of Palestinian Judaism; he was not a pure Essene, not a pure Pharisee,[4] and certainly not a pure Sadducee or Temple official. His teaching has traces of all these, but blended in a way that seems unique. It is possible to imagine the role of his mother in forming him as a teacher, and I return to this notion in Chapter 12.

Scriptural knowledge and argument

A teacher reading Jesus' uses of Scripture is inevitably going to ask what is going on, how Jesus' understanding challenges his learners, and what is the ideational structure in the way they and he think about the text. Challenge comes through in parables and interchanges with his questioners. The nature of the parables and challenges owes much to Jewish Scripture, in particular to quest narratives.[5]

Jesus condemned his generation for being childishly contrary and inconsistent with the learning they had.[6] He repeatedly appealed to or tested his hearers' knowledge of the law – 'What is written in the Law? What do you read there?'[7] – an important step that a teacher would notice, bringing to mind the learner's knowledge and awareness before taking them on to the next step. In this case the next step was to his most shocking parable, the Good Samaritan.

On some occasions Jesus used Scripture to confute Scripture – or rather, to confute his accusers' use of Scripture. Luke draws a Christological lesson from one such confutation, a skirmish with the Pharisees over picking corn on the sabbath.[8] The immediate lesson is that 'the Son of Man is master of the sabbath',[9] but there are equally important hermeneutical and pedagogical lessons to be drawn. The Torah, if used crudely, is a dangerous, inconsistent implement. As a weapon it can go off in the attacker's hands, and here it does just that. The lesson is that learners should do more than simply learn how to quote specific bits of the text. It should not be used for literalistic micro-monitoring of one's own or others' behaviour. We sense here that Jesus had somewhere learnt a big, important lesson about the Torah: that it is to be read with wisdom, keeping one's eyes on the larger narrative. Jesus won that altercation, and several others, by counter-quoting; but perhaps he might not have been fully satisfied with his victory. The eschatological figure who is the master of the sabbath is someone who has been most forcefully struck by the depths of the Torah, and is impatient with its superficial use.

There are other instances of confrontations with bits of text as a weapon. After his parable of the vineyard tenants, intended as a prediction of his rejection and death, he posed the question of eschatology and judgement. His hearers replied that a punishment is just. Jesus then used scriptural quoting to apply their moral judgement back to them.[10] There was an edge to his questioning: 'Have you *never read* in the Scriptures ...?' Never? *Oudepote* is a strong, absolute form of negative, while *anegnote*, from the verb *anaginosko*, can mean to read, or to read in public worship, and is related to getting acquainted. Jesus intended his question to be about more than familiarity with the text: he was implying that they might know it, but have not absorbed it. He was criticizing a deficiency in knowledge, certainly, but also perhaps a failure in their ritual duties towards the Torah, and an underlying lack of reflective understanding.

The sense that there was something educationally amiss in his hearers also comes up in episodes where he seized on the insights of children and compared them favourably with the poor understanding shown by adults. When the children shouted 'Hosanna to the Son of David', making the authorities indignant, he affirmed their utterance with a ready quotation from Wisdom literature.[11]

There is more educational contestation to be seen in the exchange with the Pharisees on the subject of divorce. Ostensibly it was about divorce, but under the surface was the recurrent issue of interpreting the Torah; they intended to test him on how to use the Scripture correctly, and who had the authority to do so.[12] The structure of the exchange is suggestive, again, of a larger narrative in Jesus' mind – larger than the single ethical issue of divorce. The Pharisees' question on divorce was answered by Jesus with a reference to creation, which is a higher-order theological concept than marriage or divorce. Working from creation, Jesus then appealed to a high notion of conjugality as a very important part of the created order. In effect he secured a superior position in the argument by going back to the beginning.

(We should note in passing how this exchange is misused in contemporary church discussions on marriage, divorce and same-sex marriage. The single sentence, 'This is why a man must leave father and mother, and cling to his wife, and the two become one body',[13] is taken out of context as an assertion that marriage can *only* be between a man and a woman. There are those who read this text as a foundation stone of the notion of male–female complementarity in marriage, without which marriage cannot be real or divinely approved. Male–female complementarity was certainly *presumed* by Jesus, but was it the *essence* of his argument in this text? Jesus' point is that marriage is part of the created order, indeed it changes the created order by making two into one; and the exchange as a whole is not about marriage, or complementarity, or divorce, or sexuality, it is about 'Have you not read …?',[14] it is about the use and abuse of the Torah. The horrible irony is that those who in our own time assert the text's restrictive intention on marriage *for men and women only* may be committing exactly the same hermeneutical blunder that Jesus was criticizing. They are arguing over something that is not there. They have failed to follow Jesus as a teacher at this point. However, our main intent here is not to discuss marriage, but to insert ourselves into the educational and hermeneutical dialectic under the surface.)

His questioners then counter with a scriptural incident contradicting Jesus' high notion. He reasserts his doctrine, with one important exception. In a private conversation with the disciples, he appears to concede that his teaching makes high demands and is not for everyone.[15] In Chapter 9 I shall suggest more about Matthew's filter of purity and impurity, inclusion and exclusion, which seems to rear its head at this point and elsewhere.

In this skirmish, the two sides might be said to have faced off evenly. Jesus does not seem to be entirely the victor in terms of correct use of the Torah. He has defended a hard and high interpretation, quite a puritanical and other-worldly one; he has been challenged, and has modified his position somewhat. The episode is inconclusive. Yet it illustrates the recurrent point that the Torah is a complex and difficult tool to wield.

Marriage comes up again when the Sadducees pose a question to test him.[16] It is a technical legal problem, involving seven brothers who die in sequence, all of them having married the same woman; a case of such improbability (not to mention sexism) as to be absurd. Jesus' dismissal is robust, bluntly exploding the legal question itself as well as the poor theological understanding behind it. 'You are wrong, because you understand neither the Scriptures nor the power of God.'[17] As with the Pharisees, Jesus positions himself in a higher-order theological concept, this time resurrection. We note with interest that he does not here commit himself on the truth or otherwise of resurrection; he merely deploys the concept.

In both instances, Jesus' rebuke teaches that detailed pieces of legal text in the Torah must be interpreted in the light of the larger picture, the grand narrative of theology; and the understanding of them must be shaped by realizing who God is. With the Sadducees, Jesus' reference point is God's self-revelation to Moses, a moment of drama and enormous theological potency for Israel.[18] This reference becomes his battering-ram for demolishing the entire structure of their assumptions. He destroys their premise that the technical legal question is of any worth, and he renders redundant their assumption that the Torah exists to resolve such questions authoritatively. Again, while the content of the exchange is legal and ethical, the underlying lesson is hermeneutical and educational: the wrong questions are being asked. Start again. God is God. 'And his teaching made a deep impression on the people who heard it.'[19]

Small text, big picture

Jesus' rebukes and rebuttals come up in the context of criticism and attack. In all the Gospels we see a growing conflict over his authority to teach and interpret the Torah. Matthew's Gospel accentuates this theme, latching it on to signs of the kingdom, while Jesus' critics wield the weapon of law to denounce his words and deeds. Repeatedly, Jesus wants them to learn the meaning not only of the specific words but of the Torah itself.[20] His repeated instruction to go and learn – the verb *mathein*, from *manthano*, to learn, to discover or learn by experience – is a challenge to the separation between rabbinical disciplines and the realities of life lived under the reign of God.

To sum up so far: Jesus brings a specific teacherly craft to questions of the text. He believes in detailed knowledge of the Torah, and can deploy it with textual accuracy and theological depth. He wants to shift the focus from legal to spiritual, from a sense of imposed duty to one of owned conviction, and from isolated chunks of text to the grand narrative. He knows that the Torah is full of surprises – messages that upset people's accustomed ways of thinking about God. He realizes that it is not just how people are living that is problematic, but also how they are reading and understanding the principal source of their religious life. Their theological logic is on the wrong settings.

When we wonder where Jesus 'trained', some scholars suggest that his 'missing' years must have been highly significant.[21] That he was steeped in the rabbinic tradition of scriptural knowledge, commentary, question and answer, and disputation, is very evident from his teaching style and the accounts of his contestation with hearers and the authorities. Specific parallels between his parables and epigrams and those of Rabbi Hillel, to take one example, are clear.[22] In the rabbinic tradition, a passion for Scripture and for a spiritual life based in widespread, synagogue-based knowledge of the Torah made rabbis distinctive. Jesus as a teacher focused on Scripture's grand narrative of God, and used the rabbinical techniques of dialectic and refutation to open up a text.[23] But there is another dimension to his teaching persona – one that combines rabbinical knowledge with a capacity to stand outside the mainstream and bring surprises to his learners.

The Essenes

After the Pharisees and Sadducees, the Essenes were the third important philosophical grouping within Palestinian Judaism. Over the past 70 years, since the discovery of the Dead Sea scrolls, a theory has emerged that Jesus might have been influenced by the Essene community, either at Qumran or elsewhere. What we know of the Essenes matches some key aspects of Jesus' approach to teaching.[24] They were a holiness and perfection community, mystical, other-worldly, some of them celibate and world-denying. They lived with messianic expectation, and practised baptism and perhaps even a form of ritual bread-sharing that may have had some bearing on Jesus' last meal with his disciples. Jesus' hard and high doctrine on marriage might have originated in Qumran. His focus on the inner life and on correcting wrong theological logic, and his quirky inversions, might have a credible origin in the other-worldly mysticism and wisdom culture of Qumran; and the resemblance is particularly pronounced in the Sermon on the Mount.[25] He may have experienced the Essene life directly or through John the Baptist. The apocalyptic tone that John and Jesus shared, which imposed on their followers a strong sense that truth and knowledge rested within the community, intersects with Qumran's rules of membership in a 'remarkably similar' way.[26]

So an exciting, articulate, biblically literate teacher, trained in rabbinic dialectics and immersed for a while in world-denying mysticism, begins to make himself heard and felt, and attracts the respect of the crowds.

In focusing repeatedly on learning the meaning of the words, Jesus demonstrates an enormously important teaching principle. To set people free from ignorance and dependence, teach them how to use the language. Changing the way people use and think about the language of the text amounts to giving them significant influence. In our own time, a religious education theorist has likened his subject to a second language, in which the 'most important words are usually the most ambiguous in their usage ... The ambiguity is precisely what is worth arguing about.'[27] And, borrowing from the poet Robert Frost, he observes that 'whoever controls the words controls the world'.[28]

But Jesus was not only the controller and deployer of words and texts. He acquired the knowledge and wisdom, certainly; but in his wisdom dimensions he was also *acquired by* the knowledge, just as speech 'acquires' us before we are aware of the process occurring.[29]

Conclusion

Jesus went – somewhere – and learnt the meaning of the words, the power of the Torah, its capacity to corrupt and to redeem. He learnt how to 'challenge a naive ideological enclosure'[30] in the reading of texts. He provoked direct cognitive conflict, juxtaposing received meanings with fresh ones while remaining deeply orthodox. He fought against dependency on micro-texts, against the domestication of the divine and the suppression of surprise. If the 'wings of surprise have been clipped by those who want to make the Bird of Heaven an aviary',[31] then Jesus was the one who opened the netting to let divine meaning fly free.

Notes

1 Paul Minear, 1984, *Matthew, the Teacher's Gospel*, London: Darton, Longman and Todd.

2 Matthew 13.53–58; see also Mark 6.1–6; Luke 4.16–24.

3 Chris Keith, 2011, *Jesus's Literacy: Education and the teacher from Galilee*, Edinburgh: T&T Clark.

4 Leander E. Keck, 2000, *Who is Jesus? History in perfect tense*, Columbia, SC: University of South Carolina Press, p. 53.

5 John Dominic Crossan, 2012, *The Power of Parable: How fiction by Jesus became fiction about Jesus*, London: SPCK.

6 Luke 7.31–35.

7 Luke 10.26.

8 Luke 6.3.

9 Luke 6.5.

10 Matthew 21.42–43.

11 Matthew 21.16; Wisdom 10.21.

12 Matthew 19.1–9.

13 Matthew 19.5, quoting from Genesis 2.24.

14 Matthew 19.5.

15 Matthew 19.10–12.

16 Matthew 22.23–33.

17 Matthew 22.29.

18 Exodus 3.6.

19 Matthew 22.33.

20 Matthew 9.13.

21 Bruce Chilton, Craig Evans, and Jacob Neusner, 2002, *The Missing Jesus: Rabbinic Judaism and the New Testament*, Leiden and Boston, MA: Brill.

22 Chilton, Evans and Neusner, 2002, p. 51.

23 Peter Shafer, 2014, *The Jewish Jesus: How Judaism and Christianity shaped each other*, Princeton, NJ: Princeton University Press.

24 John Bergsma, 2019, *Jesus and the Dead Sea Scrolls: Revealing the Jewish roots of Christianity*, London: Random House.

25 John Kampen, 2019, *Matthew Within Sectarian Judaism*, Hartford, CT: Yale University Press.

26 Kampen, 2019, p. 205.

27 Gabriel Moran, 1989, *Religious Education as a Second Language*, Birmingham, AL: RE Press, p. 11.

28 Moran, 1989, p. 12.

29 Moran, 1989, p. 23.

30 John Hull, 1985, *What Prevents Christian Adults from Learning?*, London: SCM Press, p. 80.

31 Hull, 1985, p. 223.

7

You have heard it said:
A teacher of hermeneutics

Introduction

Matthew's Jesus was a teacher of the Torah, but with a twist: his utter faithfulness to its text, and to the divine demands it placed, led him to strange and fateful statements, to breakthroughs and confrontations.

What we make of a teacher who repeatedly seems to say, in effect, 'the rules say this, but I say that', depends on an authentic understanding of his language and context. For some interpreters, the 'You have heard it said ... but I say ...' texts imply the inferiority of Judaism[1] – or, more precisely, an early church intent to imply it. According to that argument, Jesus, the embodiment of the new law of love, takes it upon himself to supersede the commandments of the old; his teachings are intended to replace the Torah, or to fulfil it because it is incomplete. A hermeneutical frame of binaries is in operation – inadequate vs perfect, provisional vs complete – so that surface or literal or legalistic meaning is habitually contrasted with a deeper, spiritual reading, and laid in parallel with Old and New Testaments. This outlook, which Jews refer to as supersessionism or replacement theology, and which they hold to be a teaching of contempt, is far from any responsible reading of the text; yet it is reproduced in some sermons and in popular understanding. What should we make of this?

The rabbinical method at work in 'You have heard it said ...'

Matthew arranges some epigrammatic teachings of Jesus into an extended text, the Sermon on the Mount,[2] in which we find six 'You have heard it said ... but I tell you ...' sayings, all following the same basic verbal formula.[3] The Jerusalem Bible renders *ekousate* (you have heard) as 'you have learnt', but acknowledges that learning in synagogues was oral, meaning that the tradition was passed on by saying, hearing and repeating. The root verb, *akouo*, means to hear, give heed, or understand. To each heard or spoken piece of teaching – covering six ethical questions on murder, adultery, divorce, oaths, revenge, and love of neighbour – Matthew has Jesus add a rider. The structure is regular: the given scriptural ethic, the new injunction from Jesus, two or three illustrations of the point, often very vivid and hyperbolic (for example, 'if your right eye should cause you to sin, tear it out'[4]), ending with a final injunction.[5] Sometimes we get the sense that Jesus' colourful illustrations might be case studies for discussion, or provocative questions to test his hearers' response to the new teaching and their understanding of its reasons and applicability.

The sequential structure is a rhythm, replicated in the repeated assonance of Greek words – *ekousate* (you have heard), *ego de lego* (but I tell you, or I assert, or I mean) – so that it is possible to imagine an authorial intention to imitate the call and response technique of oral teaching.

Here we are concerned not primarily with the content of Jesus' ethical teaching but with the cognitive process in Jesus the teacher's mind, and the educative experience of the hearers of what must certainly have started as an oral tradition. In passing, however, we can note that Jesus' ethical demands went higher and deeper than the given scriptural ethic. Matthew's intention, often referred to as the higher standard, offers 'a new attitude, a new spirit, a new vision ... poetical, dramatic, and pictorial'.[6] The higher standard suggests a causal relationship between key behaviours and blessedness, so that those who follow the new ethic will, despite appearances and expectations, be rewarded. The exact timing of the reward – whether in Jesus' lifetime or after the resurrection, or at some other eschatological point – is vague in the text.[7] But what is definite is the repeated sense of teaching a primitive ecclesiology to a community of people marked out and ethically separate, that they are salt and light.

Changing the hermeneutic rules

Jesus may have been doing more than suggesting a new ethical standard: he may have been challenging a hermeneutic. The Aramaic in which Jesus might have spoken the epigrams would have included, for 'said', the word *amar*, which can also mean to tell or declare. Thus Jesus might be understood as saying that others have interpreted Scripture to mean this; but I interpret it to mean that.

We may be reading a clash of worldviews in which Jesus' main mission was to challenge a way of interpreting Scripture, and augment it with a deeper and fuller understanding of God's demands. By his epigrammatic sayings, as well as his parables and healings on the sabbath, Jesus appears to have been 'subversive and provocative ... an authoritative teacher who challenges a society's leadership with its own texts'.[8] A particular interpretation, promoted by the authorities, had gradually gained hegemony in synagogues and among rabbis. Jesus' interpretation was counter-hegemonic, taking apart the dominant worldview as to the correct interpretation of text and law, and offering by word and deed a challenging alternative. As a set of ethical and interpretive precepts, as a polemic, the Beatitudes mark out Jesus' followers as completely distinct from their surrounding context.[9] In this sense, Matthew's community held Jesus to be not only a teacher of a new morality but also – and perhaps in the long term more powerfully – a new hermeneutic.

Ted Newell's theory of a new, subversive worldview helps to bring coherence to a handful of other *lego* (I tell you) statements and some miracles. Elsewhere in the Sermon on the Mount, Jesus enjoins trust in divine providence by drawing a comparison between his hearers and the lilies of the field or the birds of the air. The rhetorical pattern is similar to the six statements discussed earlier. The theological argument is more developed: if God looks after the smallest and simplest creatures, how much greater will God's providence be for you. The repetition of 'I tell you' and 'Yet I tell you' is the pivot of the argument, tilting the hearers from smaller to greater realizations, from (in Newell's usage) hegemonic to counter-hegemonic outlooks. A similarly pivotal use of *lego* occurs again later, when Matthew has Jesus once more attacking not only the content but the theological logic of his critics.[10]

The Gospels make much of whether or not Jesus challenged the law, and whether he broke the law or fulfilled it; and later, Paul was to plough himself into heavy soil on the same subject. An encompassing argument that Jesus taught a new way of interpreting Scripture, one developed in faithfulness to Israel's love of the Torah, might help to bring some unity to his words and deeds. Healing on the sabbath, overcoming taboos such as menstruation, inverting servant/master relation-ships, and cleansing the temple might all be taken as actions that go beyond the binary of obedience and disobedience. The actions have symbolic power and suggest a different, prophetic, provocative reading of the traditional teaching, but not a breach. In this account, going deeper or higher into the spirit of the law through word and deed is a modelling of the kingdom. It is exceeding the righteousness of the scribes and Pharisees by submitting to the will of God in ways that go beyond the letter of the law.[11] Moral agency becomes at once more strict (because Jesus' precepts demand radically more) and also more empowering (because the letter of the law can sometimes be broken and must sometimes be obeyed – and individuals must interpret by reading the signs of the times). Within the overarching kingdom taught by Jesus, the task of ethical interpretation has been revolutionized and made more complex, becoming subject to eschatological perspectives on what the kingdom of God requires.

The remainder of Matthew 5—7 is a collection of sayings on the good life. The sayings are densely packed with embedded quotations from Jewish Scripture. It has been noted how like a teacher Matthew is, and how teacher-like his Jesus appears. His style here particularly is compressed, concentrated, and in some ways uncategorizable.[12] The quotations come with repeated inversions or skewings of norms. What emerges from the rhetorical style is a teaching purpose to use his own and his hearers' familiarity with Scripture to penetrate to an inner meaning in which actions can mask many divergent intentions, and in which the intentions are the main point. The full dexterity of the sayings is only apparent when the scriptural base is known and considered. What brings the entire passage to its conclusion is the metaphor of the house built on sand. If the passage as a whole is about hermeneutics and prophetic interpretation as much as it is about ethics, could that hold true for the final metaphor too?

Therefore, everyone who listens[13] to these words of mine and acts on them will be like a sensible man who built his house on rock ... But everyone who listens to these words of mine and does not act on them will be like a stupid man who built his house on sand.[14]

Or, as he might have said: everyone who dares to interpret our law, and to live life, with the full depth and adventurousness that I have shown, will be wisely building on firm foundations; but everyone who chooses to remain with the dominant ways of interpreting our law will be like a fool, whose ethical effort is wasted.

This in itself is an inversion of the hegemonic view that any teaching which lacks precise moral certainty on what is permitted and what is proscribed will inevitably lead to a decline in moral standards. Matthew's Jesus, in his teachings on interpretation, absolutely contradicts it: free your interpretation and deepen your commitment.

A new community of theological practice

Arguments over whether Jesus loosened or tightened the law, broke it or upheld it or fulfilled it, continue to this day.[15] Matthew's Jesus did all this, because he brought not only a new ethical teaching that 'made a deep impression on the people' but also a new way of interpreting the law, which he 'taught ... with authority'.[16] The same Jesus who warned of a narrow gate and a hard road[17] also condemned the scribes and Pharisees, who 'shut up the kingdom of heaven in men's faces, neither going in yourselves nor allowing others to go in who want to'.[18] The same teacher, describing how to find the kingdom, how to interpret the way, warned that it was difficult, and condemned the intellectual guardians who made it more difficult still.

In repeatedly uttering, 'You have heard it said ... but I tell you ...', Matthew's Jesus was not only a prophetic ethical and hermeneutic teacher, he was also using the cultural capital of the Torah in a particular way to establish a new community of ethical and interpretive practice. He was teaching *theological method* as well as *ethical content*. The ethical teaching could not have survived scrutiny without the interpretive method to underpin it. His emerging conflict with the authorities, which Matthew presents in successive chapters, was as much about method as content. Jesus needed to make sure that his teaching would change the hearers not solely in regard to the ethical matter under consideration, but in regard to all ethical matters; that it would set them free for the kingdom; that the norms, rhythms and repertoires of a new community of practice[19] would become widespread. Perhaps that is why he focused on ways of reading the Torah: he wanted new interpretive rules to become the 'habitus'[20] informing his hearers' ways of dealing with their inherited text, building a shared practice.

If we glimpse Jesus' teaching mind at this point, perhaps there was an intention to move his learners away from atomized ethical problems to different, larger ways of using Scripture to guide living. Is that intention also in evidence in how he taught them to pray? The focus of the Lord's Prayer was first on

God, then on the kingdom, next on daily challenges of living, and only finally on being put to the test and being freed.[21] It looks like a deliberate sequence of virtues, arranged with the most important first.[22] In prayer, action and interpretation, he seemed to be teaching them a focus on the largest things first.

Jesus taught a change to the interpretive rules, for the sake of the kingdom. He did not do this so that his new rules could stay the same, becoming over time as fixed and unhelpful as the old ones. Christian pedagogical insight suggests that a successful community of practice requires continuing change and reflection, characterized by 'ongoing renegotiation of repertoire and imagination'.[23] The 'You have heard it said ...' statements are nodal points at which all aspects of Jesus' revelation intersect and confirm each other, like all the key teaching points suddenly locking together in the learning mind: a new ethical teaching as the basis for God's kingdom of justice; a new and more complex relationship with the inherited text and culture; and the person of the authoritative teacher who reveals himself.[24] Content, method and source, operating interdependently, form a revelation and throw down a powerful challenge to hearers and critics.

If Jesus did not realize this interdependence at the start of his teaching, he came to realize it through his teaching; the parable of the rock and sand confirms it. The crisis in the way people live – an ethical crisis – is the same as the crisis in the way people interpret their text and culture – a hermeneutical crisis. They are one and the same crisis. Matthew's eschatological theme confirms that Christ is both the signpost and the solution to that crisis.[25]

The cognitive shock of Jesus' message

A crisis in ethical and interpretive life seemed unwelcome news for some of Jesus' learners. John Hull considered several factors that form blockages to adult theological learning. The assumptions that the learning of new insights is for children and not for adults, that learning denotes a deficit; that adults somehow lack authority, status, maturity or dignity if they are asked to learn new ways, are all ideas that run very deep now as then, and distort ways of seeing and hearing Christ.[26] Hull offers canonical and non-canonical instances of how adults in Israel might feel belittled by a new teacher who required them to question their ways of life and their ways of interpreting a Scripture they believed they already knew well. He argues that the same imbalance between teacher and learners pertains in contemporary churches: 'So it is that learning becomes a childish activity, a mark of immaturity. To be a learner is to be in a position of inferiority; to be an adult learner is, to some extent, to abandon one's adulthood.'[27]

Did Jesus find, when teaching new ways of interpreting the Torah and new ethics, that his learners felt belittled? This depends very much on how we understand *ego de lego*, and whether we take the repeated formula as an act of telling or an act of discovery. Reception of challenging new ideas was defined by the educationalist Jerome Bruner in two ways: by assimilation of new cognition to existing mental or emotional schemata, and by accommodation of the schemata to the structure of the new information. While the latter feels more authentic to the radicalism of Jesus, and particularly to the urgency of the inbreaking kingdom, in practice 'all learning is a balance between assimilation and accommodation'.[28] But if a theological tradition and culture has become stuck in static definitions, if it has become an unlearning environment, then it is perhaps natural that adults will default to assimilation modes of learning, and will feel cognitive shock when confronted with new ways of reading their culture. New religious learning in such situations involves having to accommodate, to change their internal structures, so becomes risky and painful: 'the inhibitions, the doubts, the low morale and the fear of further cognitive shock' might make learning a 'fearful prospect' for many adults.[29]

Hull also challenges the notion that the universe of knowledge is fixed and static. Even Jesus, he suggests, did not hold that static notion; and even the creator, looking on created things, was full of surprise and delight.[30]

Beyond ethics and hermeneutics, was the Jesus of 'You have heard it said ...' also, then, a teacher of epistemology? A teacher announcing, with surprise and delight, that knowledge of God is not limited and fixed, but limitless and changing? To interpret his teaching in this way seems consistent with his messages on sin and forgiveness, as Hull proposes:

> In a universe capable of creativity, surprise is all around us, if we can but see it ... To believe in surprise is to have faith in a world where we are not entirely the slaves of our sinful past but are capable of being renewed. Love is surprising. It is surprising to be loved. Forgiveness is surprising ... To be surprised is to announce that we believe in the new birth.[31]

The eschatological dynamism of Jesus' teaching was potent then and remains so now, not least because even while it calls for radical change in ethics, interpretation and theory of knowledge about God, still it rests on an absolute, radical trust in God, a trust that reaches deeper and wider than the ties of blood, locality or tradition. It is a trust enshrined in the communities of people who have learnt something of the kingdom and are trying to live it.[32]

Notes

1 Bruce Chilton, Craig Evans and Jacob Neusner, 2002, *The Missing Jesus: Rabbinic Judaism and the New Testament*, Leiden and Boston, MA: Brill, p. 50.

2 Matthew 5.1—7.29.

3 Matthew 5.21–48.

4 Matthew 5.29.

5 W. D. Davies and D. C. Allison, 1988, *A Critical and Exegetical Commentary on the Gospel According to St Matthew*, Edinburgh, T&T Clark, pp. 548–9.

6 Davies and Allison, 1988, p. 566.

7 William C. Mattison III, 2017, *The Sermon on the Mount and Moral Theology: A virtue perspective*, Cambridge: Cambridge University Press, p. 38.

8 Ted Newell, 2009, 'Worldviews in collision: Jesus as critical educator', *Journal of Education and Christian Belief* 13(2), pp. 141–54, p. 145.

9 John Kampen, 2019, *Matthew Within Sectarian Judaism*, Hartford, CT: Yale University Press, p. 68.

10 Matthew 21.28–32.

11 Matthew 5.17.

12 R. France, 1989, *Matthew: Evangelist and teacher*, Downers Grove, IL: Inter-Varsity Press, pp. 135, 306.

13 The Greek word is *akouei* – the same root as 'hears' and 'heard'.

14 Matthew 7.24–26.

15 Mattison, 2017, pp. 65ff.

16 Matthew 7.28–29.

17 Matthew 7.13–14.

18 Matthew 23.13.

19 E. Wenger, 1999, *Communities of Practice*, Cambridge: Cambridge University Press.

20 D. Smith and K. Smith (eds), 2011, *Teaching and Christian Practices: Reshaping faith and learning*, Grand Rapids, MI: Eerdmans, p. 11.

21 Matthew 6.9–13.

22 Mattison, 2017, pp. 250ff.

23 Smith and Smith, 2011, p. 221.

24 Joseph Ratzinger, 2007, *Jesus of Nazareth*, London: Bloomsbury, p. 102.

25 David Sim, 1996, *Apocalyptic Eschatology in the Gospel of Matthew*, Cambridge: Cambridge University Press.

26 John Hull, 1985, *What Prevents Christian Adults from Learning?*, London: SCM Press, pp. 199ff.

27 Hull, 1985, p. 208.

28 David Heywood, 2004, *Divine Revelation and Human Learning: A Christian theory of knowledge*, Aldershot: Ashgate, p. 31.

29 Hull, 1985, p. 133.

30 Hull, 1985, p. 223.

31 Hull, 1985, p. 223.

32 Geza Vermes, 2003, *The Authentic Gospel of Jesus*, London: Allen Lane, p. 391.

8

Destroy this temple: The significance of location in Jesus' teaching

Introduction

What and where was the proper locus of teaching about the kingdom? With Jesus, a sense of place and setting for his teaching – where the Gospel sources placed him – was nearly always significant, and connected to what he taught, why, and with what authority.

Many Christians are attracted to the idea of Jesus as the itinerant rabbi, going where the spirit moved him, as if the locations for his work were a small detail. He was itinerant, but the places have symbolic power, and they indicate the intention of Jesus and his early followers to shape the notion of his teaching authority in a new way.

Jesus taught in the temple, in various synagogues, in the open air, under fig trees, in fields, on hilltops, by or on lakes, and in homes. Each of these locations became a classroom, temporary yet invested with that distinctive concentration of speaking, listening, questioning and action, an atmosphere that belongs always to places of learning. Many of Jesus' classrooms already had significance for Israel's shared imagination before he visited them.

Temple

The temple, the second in Israel's history, was a supreme focus of love, loyalty and sacrifice, as well as a centre of legal expertise and political leadership. Its history made it, as a building, as a site, as an idea, lustrous and potent. The temple's history had cycles of good times and bad – contamination and purification, plunder and restoration, destruction and reconstruction – which made it an emotional raw nerve, to a considerable extent inextricable from Jewish identity. In Jesus' time, the second temple was 500 years old, although it had been substantially rebuilt by Herod the Great as recently as 20 BCE. Its final destruction in 70 CE was a catastrophic trauma, the loss of their holy place.

In locating and reflecting on Jesus' classrooms we need to be particularly mindful of the temple's final destruction and its likely effect on the primitive Christian communities whose preaching shaped the Gospels. Although some Gospel material was probably written down before 70 CE, most of it came after the destruction.[1] The earliest Christian communities therefore remembered Jesus through the lens of that destruction, for good or ill. We can never be certain how much temple discourse, and anti-temple preaching, was projected back into the Gospel accounts as a result of the events of 70 CE. There was probably some projection, but it is unlikely that all the incidents involving Jesus and the temple were invented.[2]

Jewish theology in Jesus' time was ambivalent about the temple. Almost as ancient as the building itself were the debates about whether God could really dwell there. The rabbinical tradition entertained some doubts on the matter, because God was transcendent and uncontainable.[3] The prophetic tradition intertwined mystical visions magnifying the temple's spiritual power[4] with social criticism of the ritual cult.[5] Synagogues, representing religious practice based not on sacrifice but on recitation, teaching and preaching of the Torah, had emerged in many towns and in the diaspora, to some extent replacing or reducing the importance of sacrifice. Counter-temple movements of mysticism, prophecy and radical simplicity, such as the Qumran community, were critical of the temple's concentration of power, of its rituals, wealth, and perceived double standards. It is likely that John the Baptist, and therefore Jesus, imbibed deeply from counter-temple sources.[6] Yet the eschatological, apocalyptic and messianic currents within Judaism did not belong solely to radical communities: they touched the temple too, making it a lightning rod for expectations of divine cleansing and revelation.[7]

In this complex and sensitive culture, Jesus' relationship with the temple seems, in all its love and frustration, to spring from ancient and contemporary Judaism. To him it was the classroom of classrooms, the ultimate place of learning and obedience; and it was also a den of thieves. The temple was an employer of scribes, stonemasons, priests, soldiers, and money changers. Its theological output compelled people to pay for its services, a state of complicity that would inevitably arouse the anger of a radical prophet. The narrative of Jesus' action to expel the dealers from the temple appears in all four Gospels, with variations.[8] In some forms it is referred to as a cleansing of the temple, reminiscent of one strain of eschatology in Jewish Scripture,[9] while in others it is an act prefiguring his own sacrifice on the cross.[10] Jesus' action could therefore be represented as an eschatological cleansing, or a prediction of the passion, or a prophetic prognostication of the temple's destruction – or all three. What seems likely from the synoptic Gospels is that the incident, which so angered the authorities, was a key direct trigger of Jesus' arrest, trial and execution.[11]

Jesus' radical action against the temple dealers, probably having multiple theological roots, created a crisis in his relationship with the temple. The crisis was a long time coming – longer than his earthly lifetime – and it had implications for where Jesus' teaching actions took place. The locations of his classrooms are partially determined by the temple crisis, whether we ascribe the choices to Jesus himself or to the early communities who edited their material on him. His taunt to the temple guards, arresting him for teaching blasphemy – 'I was among you teaching in the temple day after day but you never laid hands on me'[12] – suggests that he had made sincere efforts to engage with the place as a classroom, even while aware of its compromised position.

Luke places Jesus' first use of the temple as a classroom in his early adolescence.[13] In this story, Jesus aged 12 stayed behind and engaged the elders in learned conversation. The incident is not in any of the other Gospels, and is out of step with the general absence of child prodigy narratives about Jesus in the canonical Gospels. There is a hint of myth-making in its mention of a three-day search for the boy Jesus, reminding us of the three days in the tomb, and also in the resemblance to the call narrative of the boy Samuel in the temple.[14] Yet the story is also more restrained and less magical than the childhood incidents in the apocryphal Gospels. By implication, the boy Jesus was acting as a teacher towards his elders, through a method of rabbinical questioning. The doctors of the law were astounded at his intelligence and his replies. The faint suggestion in Luke is that Jesus, early in his life, had demonstrated due respect for the temple authorities, but had also surpassed them in wisdom and knowledge. Implicitly the story subverts the authority and place of the elders in the temple. The temple's eventual redundancy as a classroom seems to be suggested by Luke from the outset.

And yet it is the place for which Jesus had the deepest, most physical tenderness, even though it stoned the prophets and would violently silence his own teaching.[15] Whereas the synoptics mostly place Jesus in the temple once only, towards the final crisis of his teaching ministry, John sets five extended teaching scenes in the temple, each of them happening at a festival season, usually Passover, Dedication or Pentecost. By doing so, John suggests that Jesus was a frequent teacher there over at least a two-year period.[16] This is a plausible level of frequency: it accords with Jesus' anguished cry about 'how often' he had wanted to gather Jerusalem's children and protect them;[17] also it was appropriate for the eschatological teacher to look for and teach about God's return to the place *in situ* bringing a judgement of justice, righteousness and purification.[18] As a classroom, the temple was for Jesus a place of conflict, certainly, but also a place of repeated, loving, obedient sacrifice, central to his teaching.

Synagogues

At first, Jesus the rabbi seemed more at home teaching in synagogues. Early in his ministry, an experience of teaching in the Capernaum synagogue was wholly positive and effective: the teaching was seen as new and authoritative.[19] Later, in response to a healing miracle and some teaching, there was some criticism, but most of the people were astounded and praised God.[20] In a third synagogue appearance, the Pharisees were critical and began their plot to destroy him.[21] At the Nazareth synagogue, his teaching ran into difficulties and he was amazed at their lack of faith.[22] There are contrasting indications that synagogues were seen as fruitful classrooms; for example, when Jesus was told that a centurion had helped to build a synagogue, this counted in the man's favour;[23] and even in the rejection at Nazareth his reading and teaching were conducted with due protocol, using a scroll from the radical prophetic tradition, with an audience whose expectations and approval were high to begin with. Synagogues were initially favoured locations, well suited to his methods of question and answer, and in some places open to his teaching about the kingdom of God.

But the synagogue connections seem to have gone sour. In mid-Gospel they come to be seen as places of oppression and trial,[24] full of hypocrites;[25] the 'leaven of the Pharisees' was hypocrisy, a gap between teaching and action, and for making this accusation Jesus' followers would, he predicted, be dragged to the synagogues and authorities.[26] His discourse in the Capernaum synagogue was deemed 'intolerable language'[27] because it placed apocalyptic and sacramental imagery against the legal and ethical framework of the synagogue authorities. There followed threats by the Pharisees to expel one or more of Jesus' followers from synagogues.[28]

We might understand some of these confrontations as editorial prefiguring of the major crisis in the temple, and that Jesus' classroom settings were arranged in order to build from early rumblings in synagogues, through increasingly serious confrontations, to a climax in the temple; but this hardly persuades when we realize that synagogue and temple were far from aligned with each other in a single, coherent power structure. Archaeological and documentary evidence represents synagogues as a structure of localized and distributed power, mainly occupied with the teaching of law as it applied to familial and ethical life in communities; they were distinctly different from the more ancient and sacerdotal political and ritual centre that was the temple.[29] Matthew's Gospel in particular, with its repeated references to the boundaries between membership and opposition, may have given prominence and power to the Pharisees on account of their interest in legal definitions of righteousness.[30] Laid over these distinctions was the life of the early church, which had to resolve its internal divisions regarding the mission to Gentiles, the relationship to official Judaism at synagogue and temple levels, and the theological arguments about circumcision and dietary laws – all issues that spilled over into the formation of the Gospels.

What we know of second-temple Judaism's divisions, reproduced in primitive Christian communities, discounts the idea that synagogue and temple could have been part of a systematic conspiracy against Jesus' teaching. Nevertheless, the idea that his teaching was opposed by a legalistic mindset, one equally prevalent in both synagogue and temple, has taken deep root in some Christian thinking. Recent scholarship has rejected a 'tacit and misguided decision to abstract the historical Jesus from his Jewish context ... reinventing Jesus as one who stood opposed to Judaism and its allegedly legalistic trammels'.[31]

Textually, then, it is unlikely that the Gospel material is deliberately arranged to portray the teacher in a growing confrontation with a single authority structure. And the text itself has numerous synagogue confrontations that are definitely about something of educational substance: the threat posed to the authorities, and felt keenly by them, from Jesus' use of synagogues to teach an extra-legal Judaism, taken from the prophetic and apocalyptic currents. The content and style of the teaching, while well received at first, sat uncomfortably with the given ethos of the synagogue as classroom. Synagogues as sites of kingdom learning were tested and testing. The rejection ended up being mutual.

Wilderness

The outer limits, the desert places, were already full of religious meaning in the tradition Jesus received. The Gospels send him there early, middle and late, to learn, reflect and teach. They suggest that since temple and synagogue had failed him as classrooms, the wilderness was where he had always belonged. The wilderness was a mirror opposite of the temple, and equally ambiguous. God was equally capable of transforming the desert into fertile land,[32] and of laying waste to cultivated and developed settlements.[33] In ancient Israel the ruination of cities was felt and lamented as a divine judgement, as both the result and the sign of disfavour with God:

> See, see, we are all your people; your holy cities are a wilderness, Zion a wilderness, Jerusalem a desolation, our holy and glorious temple, in which our fathers prayed to you, is burnt to the ground.[34]

A similar significance lies in the cultivated land, and in its economic and agricultural unproductiveness as a sign from God: 'Yes, thus speaks Yahweh, "the whole land shall be laid waste, I will make an end of it once for all."'[35] God, who gave them the land, the city and the temple, is the God of creation, of all lands and cities, as well as the God of deliverance. God's power is capable of sending agricultural disaster, or preventing it. From the temple to the wilderness, the goat bearing Israel's sins is sent out under the rules for the Day of Atonement.[36] The wilderness atones for sin in a different way, receiving and cleansing that which is rejected by the temple.

The desert as a place of renewal is a *leitmotif* running through Scripture, from Moses and Aaron to Elijah to Isaiah to John the Baptist. The appearance of this radical preacher of repentance in the Judean wilderness, everything about him signalling a lifestyle and a message at the extreme edge – his clothes and diet, his harsh words animating the people – amplified his location as a metaphor of his contrast with the towns and cities from which some of his listeners had come. John's challenging teaching worked in the wilderness because his language was raw, his words were of the wild places:

> You brood of vipers, who warned you to fly from the retribution that is coming? But if you are repentant, produce the appropriate fruits ... Yes, even now the axe is laid to the roots of the trees, so that any tree that fails to produce good fruit will be cut down and thrown on the fire.[37]

The axe is the coming kingdom, the tree is teaching, fruit is deeds, and the fire is eschatological judgement. John's baptism is a fierce challenge to the temple, setting up a competitive source of forgiveness in direct defiance of the temple's sacrificial system,[38] and thus a threat to the temple financially, politically and spiritually. In this liminal and highly charged context John also criticizes the structure of theological argument, which he perceives as a blockage to justice and a blindness to God's power: 'Do not think of telling yourselves, "We have Abraham for our father", because I tell you, God can raise children for Abraham from these stones.'[39]

The rough, violent linguistic tools of the desert – vipers, axes, stones – are applied to the abstracted superstructure of established theological thought and practice. While the Gospel accounts are vague as to John's exact geographical location, they are highly specific as to the character of his landscape, and assiduous in demonstrating how the landscape seeps into his teaching. With John, teaching itself was an act as wild and violent as the landscape. John's chosen classroom, the wilderness, perfectly fitted his message. Soft clothes and palaces were a disability in learning.[40] The coming Messiah would inaugurate something far from gentle. Teaching about the kingdom was an attack on majority theological thinking. And Jesus was heir to this.

Immediately after his baptism, Jesus went into the wilderness 'to be tempted by the devil'.[41] This time, the wilderness functions not so much as a classroom as an analogue of Jesus the teacher's planning mind. We can decipher from the three temptations that he may have been thinking about power, about the use and abuse of the Torah, and about the nature of the kingdom he would be proclaiming. In the second of the temptations we see the mirror-opposite temple, again showing the strange sense that these contrasting locations call to each other in Israel's imagination. The passage also intends to reveal what kind of teacher Jesus will be: one trusting radically in the power of God rather than employing influence or privilege to manipulate his audiences. We might say that the wilderness was Jesus' training.

Cultivated places

Fig trees

Teachers and pupils often associate success with some particular classrooms and failure with others. In the Gospels there is a detectable though slight motif of the fig tree as a symbolic location for teaching. Jesus' first conversation with the disciple Nathaniel opens with, 'I saw you under the fig tree'[42] – a remark of little consequence unless the fig tree is operating as a symbol. The safety and prosperity of Israel, with 'each man under his vine and his fig tree',[43] is a recurrent sign of blessing. The discovery of grapes and figs in the wilderness stands in for the existence of Israel among the nations.[44] If the figs increase abundantly, that is God's blessing;[45] if they wither or fail, it is a withdrawal of God's protection.[46] The priestly figure of Joshua, a figure of purity and salvation, was a sign of a coming time of justice and obedience to God's will. Joshua was a messianic figure whose servants would assemble under the fig tree and the vine.[47] In the Jewish imagination and culture Jesus grew up in, fig trees represented tranquillity and prosperity; they were places of assembly and conversation; they were Israel's communal and economic life. Where fig trees are abundant, communities prosper and enjoy the stability in which the Torah can be handed down, studied, reflected on. When a fig tree yields its harvest, this is Israel yielding the fruit of good actions. Between the planting of the tree and its growth and harvest, there must be the absorption of goodness, the process of learning, which needs to happen in peace. The disciple Nathaniel was paid a high compliment by being associated with a fig tree. He was being praised as an example of Israel's communal life of learning and good action.

The fig tree turned, however, from positive to negative in the classroom imagery around Jesus. Shortly before his arrest, Jesus tested the fig tree and finding it unfruitful caused it to be withered.[48] With the benefit (or disability) of hindsight, normal interpretations hold that the fig tree at this point stands in for Israel, and was judged because Jesus knew of his coming death. While the equivalence with Israel is consistent with the Torah's references, its simplicity in this particular text misses some precision and nuance. What happened between the two encounters with the fig tree – probably 24 hours apart – was that Jesus experienced frustration and anger in the temple, and his teaching authority was questioned. Therefore the trigger of the withering was his audience's failure to learn, and the temple authorities questioning his authority to teach.

But what stands out oddly in this story is Mark's throwaway comment that it was not even the season for figs.[49] To expect the tree to yield fruit then was, to put it mildly, unreasonable – unless larger things were at stake. 'But what if God is hungry? … What if, like Mark's Jesus, he cannot be doing with our prevaricating failure to make a place where all nations can pray?'[50] The challenge to his teaching continues after the fig tree incident, becoming more tense, and is met with his parable of the tenants in the vineyard.[51] The tree at this point symbolizes Israel itself, but also a blockage to learning, a universally human hard-heartedness and refusal to learn and change.

Vineyards

Vineyards are a more developed and prominent metaphor of Israel. Like fig trees, they are symbols of prosperity, of God's favour. Their failure and destruction are signs of disfavour.[52] The vineyard is faithful Israel and faithless Israel. If Jesus taught in the cultivated places, the fields and villages, he would have been in or near vineyards. In his imagery, vineyards became places that spoke about a test of learning, and ultimately about its failure. The Isaiah theme of the beloved friend's vineyard – 'Let me sing to my friend the song of his love for his vineyard'[53] – was a repeated lament in Jewish Scripture,[54] to which Jesus added only a little in terms of plot. Jesus used the same plot features – planting, flourishing, growth, broken hedge, destruction, labourers. But in his hands the vineyard became a sharper crisis text, a judgement of learning about the kingdom. In Isaiah the threat of destruction – hedges removed, rain withheld – was a general comment on Israel; for Jesus the threatened vineyard became a specific test of people's reception of him and his message,[55] describing a long-term failure to learn. The tenants did not understand their relationship to the place, or to the messengers. The owner, by contrast, learnt bitterly and all too well, making an end to the tenants and giving the vineyard to others. The parable about the vineyard labourers who demand differential wages[56] was a teacher's protest against those who wished to force distinctions between better and worse.

The judgement on learning was sometimes delayed – a fig tree was given one more year to make progress and bear fruit[57] – but in the end destruction came.

The temple was destroyed, synagogues condemned. 'Make a tree sound and its fruit will be sound; make a tree rotten and its fruit will be rotten. For the tree can be told by its fruit.'[58]

Classrooms of crisis

In the end, and shockingly, not just trees and vines but all sites of learning came to destruction either by deed or word, and became a wilderness. Jesus brought crisis to teaching: the Gospels placed him in classroom after classroom, none of them able to contain him or withstand him. Just as rabbis had debated whether or not God could dwell in the temple, yet still revered it, so Jesus' teaching called into question every classroom, yet still remained located and rooted in those places. And just as John the Baptist's violent verbal attacks on normal cognition, normal theology, had blown in from the wilderness, so Jesus' eschatology blew apart the places he and his people used for their imagery and daily life. Jesus' chosen classrooms were without exception dangerous, explosive places.

Notes

1 Ben Blackwood, John Goodrich and Jason Maston (eds), 2018, *Reading Mark in Context: Jesus and second temple Judaism*, Grand Rapids, MI: Zondervan.

2 Simon Joseph, 2018, *Jesus and the Temple: The crucifixion in its Jewish context*, Cambridge: Cambridge University Press.

3 Exodus 25.8; 1 Kings 8.27.

4 Isaiah 6.1ff.

5 Amos 5.21; 8.3.

6 Nick Perrin, 2010, *Jesus and the Temple*, London: SPCK, pp. 17ff.

7 Lester Grabbe, 2010, *An Introduction to Second Temple Judaism: History and religion of the Jews in the time of Nehemiah, the Maccabees, Hillel, and Jesus*, London: T&T Clark, pp. 96ff.

8 Mark 11.15–19; Matthew 21.12–17; Luke 19.45–46; John 2.13–25.

9 Malachi 3.1–3, 8–9.

10 John 2.21–22.

11 Joseph, 2018.

12 Mark 14.49; Luke 22.53.

13 Luke 2.41–50.

14 1 Samuel 3.1–10.

15 Luke 13.31–35.

16 John 2.13–25; 5.1–47; 7.2—8.20; 10.22–39; 12.12—19.26.

17 Matthew 23.37.

18 Malachi 3.1–5.

19 Mark 1.21–28.

20 Mark 2.1–12.

21 Mark 3.1–6.

22 Mark 6.1–6.

23 Luke 13.10.

24 Matthew 10.17.

25 Matthew 6.2; Mark 12.39.

26 Luke 12.1–12.

27 John 6.59.
28 John 9.22; 12.42.
29 Donald Biner and Anders Runesson, 2010, *The Ancient Synagogue from its Origins to 200 CE*, Leiden: Brill.
30 John Kampen, 2019, *Matthew Within Sectarian Judaism*, Hartford, CT: Yale University Press, p. 204.
31 Perrin, 2010, p. 2.
32 Isaiah 41.18.
33 Zephaniah 2.13; Joel 2.3; Ezekiel 6.14.
34 Isaiah 64.9–11.
35 Jeremiah 4.27.
36 Leviticus 16.5–10.
37 Luke 3.7–9.
38 Robert Webb, 2006, *John the Baptizer and Prophet: A sociohistorical study*, Eugene, OR: Wipf and Stock.
39 Luke 3.8.
40 Luke 7.24–26.
41 Matthew 4.1–11.
42 John 1.48.
43 1 Kings 4.25; Jeremiah 30.10.
44 Hosea 9.10.
45 Joel 2.21–25; Jeremiah 32.15.
46 Joel 1.1–20; Amos 4.9.
47 Zechariah 3.10.
48 Mark 11.13–14, 20–25.
49 Mark 11.13.
50 Elizabeth Templeton, 1990, 'For it was not the season for figs', in Alastair Hulbert and Peter Matheson (eds), 2019, *In Your Loving is Your Knowing: Elizabeth Templeton: Prophet of our times*, Edinburgh: Birlinn Ltd, pp. 157–60, p. 159.
51 Mark 11.27—12.12.
52 Ezekiel 28.25–26; Deuteronomy 28.30.
53 Isaiah 5.1–7.
54 Psalm 80.8–16; Hosea 10.1–4; Jeremiah 2.21–22; Ezekiel 15.1–8; 17.1–10; 19.10–14.
55 Mark 12.1–12.
56 Matthew 20.1–16.
57 Luke 13.6–9.
58 Matthew 12.33.

9

The lesson that fails: Was Matthew's Jesus a good teacher?

Introduction

It appears that Jesus was not always a successful teacher. If the measures of success include impressing the audience with his authority and helping them to understand the kingdom – measures that the Gospels frequently apply – then Jesus' record seems mixed.

Central to this is the problem of Jesus' strategy of obscurity as a teacher, which takes three general forms in the Gospel accounts. There are moments when he loses an audience, failing or even refusing to make his message clear; moments when he declines to answer a question clearly or directly; and moments when his Messiahship is denied or kept a secret. One can recognize a need for such moments in literary terms: in order to set up the dramatic tension and plot structure that would lead to the cross, some audience misapprehension and hostile criticism were editorially necessary. But the frequency of the episodes, the precision given to the theological terms of the misunderstandings, and the edge of anger with which Jesus sometimes responds, call for some educational reflection.

Does a good teacher blame his learners? For Christian preachers there is a temptation to settle this problem by allowing ourselves to assume that Jesus was exasperated by the slow-wittedness, obduracy, vested interests or enmity of his audiences; that in effect his teaching mission was not a success, and this led to Calvary. That kind of causal relationship between unsuccessful teacher and saviour is explored by Kier-kegaard.[1] It is in the end an unsatisfactory solution, as we shall see.

Careless sower, careless teacher

Mark's Gospel has Jesus teaching a large crowd by the lakeside.[2] The passage underlines the need to understand his teaching, and the expectation that people will respond in different ways. It includes an explanation of why he uses parables. Further on, Mark records that Jesus spoke in parables 'so far as they were capable of understanding it', and would speak only in parables, explaining the meaning later to his disciples when they were alone.[3] And yet in Matthew some people remarked admiringly on his wisdom and deeds of power.[4] There are several other Gospel passages in which the crowd, or the disciples, fail to understand Jesus properly. Addressing this in the Markan context, we might well observe that 'countless readers have puzzled over why the disciples ... seem so dense'.[5]

The communication of meaning in this and other parables remains problematic. If we borrow from late modern sociology the supposition that language is a communicative act, signifying in its higher and more complex forms an intent to be understood, we must ask of Jesus what his intention was in those contexts. If 'communicative intent is the fundamental form of meaning',[6] then did he intend to be understood, or to deny understanding?

The one parable that stands out as an illustration of this problem of language and meaning is the parable of the sower.[7] It stands out pre-eminently as an episode where his parable-based teaching apparently fails, like a joke that needs explaining, which he does a few verses later. This time, Jesus seems to have moved so far ahead of his learners that he is forced to go back and explain. We are familiar with this parable in the form of an allegory – a tabular device in which every element in the story has a specific meaning related to Israel, Christ, or his hearers. It apparently concerns the teaching of the word of the kingdom and the reception given to it by four different types of hearers. The fourth type, those who hear, understand and bear fruit, is preceded by three types who fail.

So we apparently have a parable about why some people don't understand Jesus' parables; a joke about why some people don't get jokes. Wrapped up in it, as the central character, is a sower who makes an elementary mistake of technique by sowing indiscriminately without first ploughing. Despite his profligate and careless casting, sowing 'with abandon',[8] he seems almost surprised when there is failure in three cases out of four.

If the central character were a teacher instead of a sower, the same allegorical structure would highlight his careless approach to ensuring learning: how with some pupils he failed to prepare, with others he neglected to support them when they were struggling, and so on. Only a quarter of his pupils make any progress: the rest fail. And yet the parable seems to invite criticism of the different types of ground/learner, rather than attributing any responsibility to the sower/teacher. Jesus, in telling a story about his own teaching, seems unconcerned: indeed, we see his projection of blame on to those of his hearers who have not grasped his meaning. 'The secret of the kingdom of God is given to you [the disciples], but to those who are outside everything comes in parables.'[9] He draws justification from the prophet Isaiah, whose harsh words[10] he applies to his own wider audience: 'the reason I talk to them in parables is that they look without seeing and listen without hearing or understanding'.[11] This explanation, given to his more successful chosen learners, begs the question why he teaches in parables, or teaches beyond his circle at all.

It is commonplace to interpret this episode as Jesus' frustrated response to people's obduracy, which is also recorded elsewhere. He refuses to give signs, and solemnly promises that 'no sign will be given to this generation'.[12] When the disciples ask why Jesus does not make his meaning clear, his answer concedes their point.[13] When warning the disciples of 'the leaven of the pharisees',[14] he fails to make his meaning understood, and criticizes them for not understanding either his signs or his sayings.[15] Jesus blesses his father for hiding things from the learned and revealing them to 'mere children',[16] which we can take to mean people who are relatively uneducated.[17] As part of Mark's 'chiasmus'[18] or contradiction pattern, opposites are held in painful tension: inside/outside, speech/ writing, presence/absence. Perhaps another such tension is understanding/misunderstanding.

Willed opaqueness and its reasons

Commenting on the sower, Joseph Ratzinger remarks on the 'willed opaqueness' of Jesus, and wonders whether it could mean that 'the parables are intended not to open doors, but to lock them'.[19] He settles for an explanation based in a doctrine of human freedom interacting with the divine word:

> Prophets fail: their message goes too much against general opinion and the comfortable habits of life. It is only through their failure that their word becomes efficacious.[20]

But this fails to explain why sometimes they do break through, why sometimes the audience does understand, and how a prophetic message *only* becomes efficacious when it is not understood. Kierkegaard also falls into this trap, by equating the teacher with divine truth and the learner with untruth and sin.[21] It is a theological catch-22: when the message works, Jesus is a great teacher; when it fails, the audience were blind or wilful, and anyway failure leads to the cross and resurrection, so all is well in the end.

When we as teachers witness the willed opaqueness of Jesus, we should be deeply perturbed by it. The wider record in the Gospels does not appear to present Jesus as a model teacher or even a particularly effective one. Dillon identifies 112 teaching episodes in the Gospels and compares how they are received by his audience. His study shows that Jesus elicits 'relatively little positive reaction',[22] and that of more than 50 parables, only five include a reaction from learners.[23] While demurring at Dillon's numerical method, Newell acknowledges that the 'naked record does not make Jesus to be the best teacher of all time, if assessment is by demonstrated learning'.[24]

It seems that a critical stance towards Jesus' apparent method in the sower episode is warranted. We are invited to cheer his story, blaming those whom he blames and identifying with those he favours. Yet the central character is far from appealing to our pedagogical experience: this sower/teacher/ joker seems to revel in how badly he performs in all three functions. Nothing works: the sowing is ineffective, the teaching is not understood, the joke against his hearers backfires on him.

For Christians there is always a temptation to cover Jesus' moral vulnerability at this point by searching around for some explanation. Any hermeneutic strategy that sets out to exonerate him invites suspicion as being too convenient. The justifications include, for example, the divine decision to harden some people's hearts and blind them to the word;[25] Jesus' need to obscure his meanings for his own safety;[26] and the idea that he spoke in parables *because* they did not understand.[27] With a teacher's mind we need to weigh these claims, with an eye on whether it seems a probable interpretation of the text or is rather more motivated by a prior hermeneutical decision that Jesus cannot be wrong or unjust. Perhaps the most problematic passage of apparent injustice is Jesus' threefold refusal to help the Syro-Phoenician woman who pleads on behalf of her daughter.[28] I examine this passage and the hermeneutic strategies people have used in order to defend Jesus in Chapter 12.

In the first chapter, I suggested that Christ is both knowable and unknowable, and any good teacher is both clear and opaque. Even so, there is surely a difference between being opaque sometimes and being determined that some learners will fail. The problem of Jesus' apparently willed and wilful obscurity, and his justification of this with resort to Scripture, presents a threat to our notion of him as an ethical teacher. We can only resolve this if we either accept that he was sometimes less than a good teacher, or find a reason – a credible reason – to understand the text in a different way and perhaps through different eyes.

If we imagine that what we are reading in the sower episode is not, as it seems, a unified and coherent account of Jesus' story, his justification of method and his interpretation, might this take us forward? The slight inconsistencies between the accounts raise the probability of editorial influence in the early church communities that shaped the Gospel literature. In educational terms, can we imagine that we are hearing the pupils' reminiscences and interpretations of a teacher rather than watching him first-hand? The disciples' social memory of their teacher, refracted through their subsequent experience of his influence, becomes perhaps our clearest way to access this text – and to understand what has happened to their memory of their teacher.[29]

A scholar with an eye for Jesus' teaching mind suggests a 'split screen' reading of allegorical material that indulges in typologies. A type in the Gospel text should be taken as referring to a specific group of people in the life of the primitive Christian community: thus the disciples correspond to leaders of churches, the crowds to lay members of churches, and the scribes and Pharisees to leaders of rival synagogues in Palestine and Syria.[30]

The treatment of the parables by Joachim Jeremias[31] places them all into the context of the primitive Christian community. The earliest Christian groups had to contend with three specific theological and ecclesiological pressures: the delay in the *parousia* that had seemed imminent in Jesus' teaching; the dispute over whether the mission should include Gentiles; and the question of how the church should be regulated and led. This third pressure created a 'transference' in which parables that had originally been addressed to Jesus' critics or to the religious leaders of Israel were now 'applied by editorial activity to the leadership of the church'.[32] Jeremias argues that such a transference was at work in the 'allegorization' of the parable of the sower; that 'on linguistic grounds alone it is unavoidable'[33] that the allegorical interpretation is not Jesus' own.

Mark began the allegorizing and Matthew used it extensively; it is possible that Matthew took Mark's allegory of the sower as his template, elaborating it and adding others.[34] Jeremias notes that allegorization is absent only in Luke's special source and the Gnostic Gospel of Thomas.[35] That a Gnostic source so predisposed to hidden meanings and dualities should leave aside any opportunity to allegorize is strongly suggestive that there was little or no allegorizing in the original material. Therefore, most of the allegorizing was not part of the original, and 'only by discarding these secondary interpretations and features can we once more arrive at an understanding of the original meaning of the parables of Jesus'.[36]

The early church dispute over whether or not the mission could be extended to the Gentiles was a dynamic issue. In Matthew's community they appear to have shifted their position from shunning Gentiles to a provisional inclusiveness in preaching to all nations.[37] A set of sharper dilemmas sits underneath this: was their teacher really a Jew, or not? Could they, who had been so changed by their teacher, call themselves Jews? Was he a strict observer of the law, or a disruptor – an insider or an outsider? What should it mean to follow a teacher who was sometimes one, sometimes the other? That tension is often near the surface in the synoptic Gospels.[38] Its potential relevance to the parable of the sower might be that they believed Jesus was leaning towards insider status at that point. But this leaves unresolved his apparent apathy about outsiders. There are parallels with the harsh treatment of the man without a wedding garment in another parable.[39] The same tension between mainstream and heterodox followers is observed among the mixed crowd of Jesus' followers in the Johannine literature.[40]

The sower allegory, if understood as primitive Christian material, provides a precise classification of types of early church member; it delineates four ways in which those members might respond to the preaching of the word. The context set by Matthew immediately preceding the sower story shows us instances of growing conflict with Jesus' critics,[41] talk of an unclean spirit at work in an evil generation,[42] and sharp divisions between those who are with Jesus and those who are not.[43] Each of these, and all of them together, could be an arrangement of instances that challenged the leaders of the early church and made them tend towards a strict classification of loyalty and identity, of the sort offered in the allegory. If the allegorization is not original, the typecasting of learners and followers is not Jesus' own, and as a teacher he is to some extent exonerated. In order to have confidence in this rebuttal, an alternative theory of Jesus' probable intention in the parable would be helpful. Jeremias suggests that, shorn of their early church allegories, Jesus' parables are eschatological calls to recognize the times and to act in response to God's generosity.[44] The sower is followed closely by parables of the darnel, the mustard seed, and the yeast,[45] each of them a tale of God's extravagant generosity and the explosive growth of the kingdom. Could the sower simply be the first in a quartet of eschatological parables of the kingdom? But the mention of four types of ground gives the sower a plot structure different from the other three, suggestive of restrictions on explosive growth.

According to the argument of Luise Schotroff, it is now possible to free ourselves from the habit of allegorizing the parables, and instead to approach them as stories that critique social structures of oppression.[46] The oppression at work here might not be Jesus'.

A group of former pupils recall a teacher's lesson at some years' distance. Some of them were not present, but all share the same current preoccupations. Over time, they impose on their memory of the teacher a neat interpretation of what went on in his classes. They codify his significance for them, continuing to reinforce this until the difference is blurred between what he actually taught them and what they now believe. This is not only possible, but pedagogically a frequent reality. This particular instance of Jesus' obscurity, if seen in this way, is perhaps less an ethical and psychological problem of the teacher, and more a feature of the role of the community who remember him and wish to own him in distinctive ways. Perhaps it is also a feature of our memory in how we recall our teacher's words and how we interpret them in our time and place. Perhaps the sower episode tells us less about Jesus the teacher than we think, but more about our reception of him as teacher and ourselves and each other as learners – more, perhaps, than we want to know.

The conundrum remains

Yet the truth about Jesus dances in and out of sight in other ways. Luke-Acts treats the question as if it were one of the giving and withholding of sight.[47] Paul's conversion makes him blind for three days, for example.[48] In Luke, Jesus's identity as king, the one destined for the throne of his ancestor David, is announced;[49] then it is obscured in a vague answer to a question about his identity;[50] then refused in a blocking answer – 'the kingdom of God does not admit of observation';[51] then raised at the moment of trial and crisis and again not answered directly;[52] and finally answered in bitter irony through the sign on the cross.[53]

The messianic secret is mentioned eight times in Mark alone.[54] If we agree that it is 'not a historical fact so much as a theological idea',[55] we might place the secret as a device to show that the risen Christ had always known about his messiahship, even though no one in his earthly life had mentioned it.

When the disciples argue among themselves about who is the greatest in the kingdom,[56] clearly even they, who are so close to Jesus, have seriously misunderstood him. The setting seems to be informal: they are together without a larger audience, they have freedom to discuss intensely, but children are playing nearby. The inversion of values in the kingdom is illustrated with the elevation of children, in their humility and ignorance, as models of understanding.

Even with all the rationalizations offered by Jesus' appeal to Scripture and by subsequent theologians, we are still left with a record of a puzzling teacher who on occasion misleads and perturbs, and is not a uniformly useful or admirable example.

Notes

1 Howard V. Hong and Edna H. Hong (eds), 1985, *Søren Kierke-gaard: Philosophical fragments*, Princeton, NJ: Princeton University Press.

2 There are fairly close parallels between Mark 4.1–20, Matthew 13.1–17 and Luke 8.4–15. Some elements also appear in Mark 8.18 and John 12.39–41.

3 Mark 4.33–34.

4 Matthew 13.54–56.

5 R. Fowler, 1992, 'Reader-response criticism: Figuring Mark's readership', in J. Anderson and S. Moore (eds), *Mark and Method: New approaches in biblical studies*, Minneapolis, MN: Augsburg Fortress Press, pp. 50–83, p. 59.

6 Anthony Giddens, 1993, *New Rules of Sociological Method: A positive critique of interpretive sociologies*, Cambridge: Polity Press, p. 96.

7 Matthew 13.4–23.

8 D. Garland, 2001, *Reading Matthew: A literary and theological commentary*, Macon, GA: Smith and Helwys Publishing, p. 147.

9 Mark 4.11.

10 Isaiah 6.9–10.

11 Matthew 13.11, 13.

12 Mark 8.12.

13 Matthew 13.10.

14 Matthew 16.5–12.

15 Garland, 2001, p. 150.

16 Matthew 11.25–27.

17 Traces of a wisdom metaphor, a divine order that gives legitimacy to his teaching, have been detected here by C. Deutsch, 1996, *Lady Wisdom, Metaphor and Social Context in Matthew's Gospel*, Valley Forge, PA: Trinity Press International, p. 142.

18 Stephen Moore, 1992, 'Deconstructive Criticism: Turning Mark inside-out', in Anderson and Moore (eds), pp. 84–102, p. 96.

19 J. Ratzinger, 2007, *Jesus of Nazareth*, London: Bloomsbury, p. 189.

20 Ratzinger, 2007.

21 Hong and Hong, 1985, p. 11.

22 J. Dillon, 1981, 'The effectiveness of Jesus as a teacher', *Lumen Vitae* 36(2), pp. 137–40.

23 Dillon, 1981, pp. 143–5.

24 Ted Newell, 2009, 'Worldviews in collision: Jesus as critical edu-cator', *Journal of Education and Christian Belief* 13(2), pp. 141–54, pp. 142–3.

25 The reference to Isaiah 6.9–10 is problematic in Matthew because there is grammatical confusion over whether the prophecy is intended to be fulfilled, or whether its fulfilment is merely observed as the accidental outcome of human will. The grammatical ambiguity is in the single word 'that' (*ina*) in Mark 4.12, which Matthew adapts. In other words, we do not know whether the hearers fail to understand Jesus because their hearts have grown coarse, or – as seems more likely in Matthew's version – their hearts have been made coarse so that they will not be able to understand him. However, in either sense we still have a dismissive and pedagogically inadequate stance.

26 Newell, 2009, p. 142.

27 Note the 'therefore' (*dia touto*) in Matthew 13.13.

28 Mark 7.24–30.

29 Anthony Le Donne, 2009, *The Historiographical Jesus: Memory, typology, and the son of David*, Waco, TX: Baylor.

30 Paul Minear, 1984, *Matthew, the Teacher's Gospel*, London: Darton, Longman and Todd, pp. 10–11.

31 Joachim Jeremias, ET 1972, *The Parables of Jesus*, London: SCM Press.

32 Jeremias, 1972, p. 66.

33 Jeremias, 1972, p. 77. His evidence is based on the unusual use of the word *logos* in verse 19, the start of the allegorical explanation. *Logos* occurs nowhere else in Matthew, but was in common use in the early church. He also points out that preaching is metaphorically represented by gathering harvest, rather than by sowing.

34 Jeremias, 1972, p. 85, fn. 92.

35 Jeremias, 1972, p. 88.

36 Jeremias, 1972, p. 89.

37 Contrast Matthew 10.5–6 with Matthew 28.19.

38 Moore, 1992, pp. 84–102.

39 Matthew 22.11–14.

40 Oscar Cullmann, ET 1976, *The Johannine Circle*, London: SCM Press.

41 Matthew 12.22ff. The conflicts were to grow more bitter and they form a long-term theme in Matthew, leading to the crisis of Jesus' arrest and trial.

42 Matthew 12.43–45.

43 Matthew 12.46–50.

44 Jeremias, 1972, pp. 115ff.

45 Matthew 13.24–33.

46 Luise Schotroff, 2006, *The Parables of Jesus*, Minneapolis, MN: Augsburg Fortress Press.

47 Beverley Roberts Garenta, 2008, 'Learning and re-learning the identity of Jesus in Luke-Acts', in B. Garenta and R. Hays (eds), *Seek-

ing the Identity of Jesus: A pilgrimage, Grand Rapids, MI: Eerdmans, pp. 148–65.

48 Acts 9.1–9.
49 Luke 1.32–33.
50 Luke 7.22–23.
51 Luke 17.20–21.
52 Luke 23.3.
53 Luke 23.38.
54 Mark 1.34; 1.43–45; 3.12; 5.43; 7.36; 8.26; 8.30; 9.9.
55 Janice Anderson and Stephen Moore, 1992, 'The Lives of Mark', in Anderson and Moore (eds), pp. 1–22, p. 6.
56 Matthew 18.1–6.

10

How shall we picture the kingdom?
Reflections on a critical incident

Introduction

'What is the kingdom of God like? What shall I compare it
with?'[1] These questions are rendered by Ronald Knox as
'What is there that bears a likeness to the kingdom of heaven;
what comparison shall I find for it?' and by the New American
Standard as 'How shall we picture the kingdom of God, or by
what parable shall we present it?' In this chapter I focus on
this double question, looking for what it suggests of Jesus as a
teacher. It is a rare instance of a public religious communicator
laying bare not only the form but the function of his work.

These questions are often passed over as the reader hurries
on to what comes next – the parables of the mustard seed growing in a garden and the woman with yeast and flour, and the
meanings derived from them. It might seem that we are being
invited to treat those two parables – both of them very short,
concentrated metaphors – as suggested *answers* to the methodological *question* of the nature of the kingdom and how it can
be described. Most commentaries focus on the parables, rather
than the moment of introspection that precedes them, and in
doing so something important is lost.

A teacher's moment of introspection

When looked at through the lens of a teacher, the double question Jesus posed – perhaps as much to himself as to anyone else – was in itself highly significant. It was more than a simple pondering over choice of metaphor; it raised deeper questions about whether the kingdom was actually explainable in words, and whether the words chosen had any prospect of being understood.

This represents a brief moment of pedagogical introspection. Why has Luke chosen to place it here? Highlighting the context, Luke begins with the significant word 'therefore' (*oun*), unusually placing it at the start of his sentence and suggesting continuity with what has gone before. From this we can suppose the question to be more than a matter of technical method in the moment: the question is somehow the result of what has just taken place.

In the pericopes leading up to the double question, Luke has arranged the material on Jesus so that a clear pattern emerges. To begin with, the ministry in Galilee is positive. There are powerful signs of God's kingdom, seen by multitudes. Herod seems puzzled, but not yet hostile. There are relatively few warnings of the suffering to come. But from the moment when Jesus 'resolutely took the road for Jerusalem',[2] we note a developing confrontation with his hearers and the teaching authorities, in which the tone of the confrontation keeps being ratcheted up.

It is possible to see this entire section of Luke as a slowly gathering crisis and confrontation over teaching. (With small differences, Matthew narrates the same escalation leading up to the same double question.) Jesus taught the kingdom to great crowds, appointed other teachers to spread his work, and warned his disciples of hardship to come. He reflected repeatedly on people's understanding, and lack of understanding.[3] He created the impression that the kingdom of God was not for everyone, and he contrasted the kingdom with images of the good life – a full barn, good clothes, filial duty, obedience to the law. At the same time, for those who would be part of the kingdom, he had words of comfort and reassurance.[4] He denounced towns that would not receive the message, denounced a whole generation, and denounced his critics. He developed his theme of criticism towards the Pharisees and lawyers,[5] attacking their hypocrisy and failure of insight in colourful, forceful terms – clean outside, dirty inside; obsessing about details while overlooking justice; pompous and arrogant; people who load up burdens and will not lift them; people who approve and benefit from the killing of the prophets; obstacles to knowledge, who will not learn and prevent others from doing so.

Jesus' language in those criticisms is highly physical – washing and dirt, tombs, spilt blood, keys, yeast – and as such it is both accessible and unambiguous. In its direct physicality, deployed as a weapon against a repeated stubbornness and failure to understand, the language is reminiscent of John the Baptist. It is clear that an apocalyptic storm is gathering, a crisis in which Jesus' teaching will be put to the test. Jesus moves from 'Anyone who is not against you is for you' to 'He who is not with me is against me',[6] suggesting that the issues raised by his teaching are becoming sharper.

Immediately before the double question, Jesus healed a woman who was crippled and could not stand straight, and he did this on the sabbath,[7] thus reigniting the long-running confrontation between him and the authorities. He challenged the idea that those on whom sudden misfortune fell must have been exceptionally wicked, replacing it with a teaching that all people were equally wicked and 'unless you repent you will all likewise perish'.[8] When he was himself challenged about healing the woman on the sabbath he accused his accusers of hypocrisy.[9] Between those two episodes, Luke inserts the parable of the fruitless fig tree whose owner gives it one more year before deciding whether or not to cut it down.[10] The significance of fig trees and other sites of failed learning is discussed in Chapter 8.

As Luke arranges them, parable, sign and argument follow each other repeatedly, so that the dramatic actions and arguments of Jesus come first, then the double question, followed by the two parables. We gain an impression of a public communicator who was working hard, was at the centre of a dramatic and tightening chain of events, and was winning some of the time – the multitude followed him and grew in number – but at the same time he was often encountering obstacles to understanding. The obstacles appeared to be of two kinds: the hypocrisy of his critics, and the underlying theological structures in the minds of many hearers.

The underlying theological structures are his hearers' assumptions and ways of thinking that darken their insight and block the path towards grasping the kingdom's significance. Luke mentions several in the chapters leading up to the double question. Why did they think that he cast out devils by the power of the prince of devils, despite this being a ridiculous theory? Why did they ask for a sign, not believing the signs already shown? Why did they want Jesus to adjudicate on specific legal or ethical points, but miss the larger picture of the coming kingdom? Why did they bless him and his mother in particular, but fail to hear his word and follow it? Why could they not use their knowledge of the Torah and prophets to read the signs of the times? Why did they not see wickedness as a widescale problem, failing to understand that God's judgement is on all? While other parts of the Gospels describe these kinds of failures as hardness of heart, or as God's decision to hide things from the wise,[11] here we see a pattern of repeated *cognitive* failure, signposted even after many signs and much teaching. The failures have something to do with a poor theological understanding of the Torah and a weak grasp of the power of God. In the sequence of incidents we sense a growing frustration in Jesus.

Is there some connection between the repeated cognitive failures, the hypocrisy of the Pharisees, and the double question? He blames the lawyers for taking away the key of knowledge, for refusing to go through the door of knowledge themselves, and preventing others from doing so.[12] The charge against them is more than double standards, then: the people's failure to understand, or to move from particulars to the general point, their weakness in reasoning from the heart of Scripture, their unwillingness to follow, all apparently stem from watching, over a long period, the authorities behaving in a similar fashion. Having experienced frustration at their effect, Jesus reaches the point of considering his own method.

We might imagine him asking: what am I trying to say about the kingdom, and am I saying it clearly enough? What can I say or do to break through into their understanding more effectively? These are questions to himself as much as, or more than, to his hearers.[13] That the questions are shared with us, the readers, shows in the mind of Luke some claim to insight into the inner workings and development of Jesus' teaching method, and furthermore an insight that he considers important enough to attend to as part of a gathering picture of a teacher in growing conflict with the authorities.

The double question is a moment of methodological introspection, a fulcrum between a teacher's action and reflection. What seems to be turning over in Jesus' mind at that point is more than function or technique, more than simply a choice of metaphors. It has implications for his sense of his mission and might suggest that his mission is shaped by his practical experience of success and frustration as a teacher. Luke's Jesus is a teacher, through deeds, thought and words. The fulcrum joins the thought to the words, showing that there is a connective meaning in Jesus' mind but also showing him struggling to convey his meaning and wondering how he can improve the clarity of his message.

A critical incident

In teachers' terms, the double question in the context described above has all the hallmarks of a critical incident. The term 'critical incident' is not intended to indicate any traumatic episode; in the educational lexicon it may be quite commonplace, but it operates on the teacher's mind to create reflection and change. A working definition of a critical incident might be an 'unplanned, unanticipated event that occurs during a lesson and ... serves to trigger insights about some aspect of teaching and learning'.[14]

These incidents can be positive, for example if learners do better than expected, or negative, if a teacher's assumptions are challenged or exposed in a way that becomes a problem. Such an incident is valuable because it is given meaning by the teacher; the same episode happening to another teacher might not be critical at all. The event is critical in the sense that it is pivotal, and prompts critical self-reflection. The teacher's planning mind chooses to make it critical. The events need not be dramatic, but they are turning points.[15]

John Mason's thinking on teachers as researchers of their own practice prompts him to offer the 'discipline of noticing'[16] as something that promotes the teacher's growth and maturation, that is a process of transformation – as distinct from tinkering or small-scale innovation. Mason describes this as 'research from the inside',[17] a 'natural and intuitive'[18] action in a good teacher. The discipline of noticing prompts the teacher to modify their practice by testing all their assertions and assumptions.

A critical incident can have emotional impact, as when a teacher is perplexed or unsettled by an experience they do not fully understand, or perhaps feels surprise, guilt, frustration, entertainment or amusement. Teachers experience a 'disequilibrium' that 'triggers the search for strategic change'.[19] They can use reflection on the incident in order to recover their sense of equilibrium.

Relying on those who have taught and observed this, we may safely say that for teachers, critical incidents

- come into view because the teacher chooses to give them significance;
- are a key element in a teacher's growth and development;
- happen more frequently to change agents;
- can be unsettling.

There seems little doubt that Jesus, the radical teacher of the kingdom, was a change agent. He was also portrayed as a teacher who noticed his learners' reactions, detected their underlying thinking, gave significance to what he noticed, and was emotionally affected by it. We are, however, left with wondering what learning for himself Jesus took from that moment.

A vulnerable teacher

If Jesus' double question can be understood as a critical incident, it is because in that moment method and message meet at a crossroads. Jesus took the 'beautiful risk'[20] of placing his message into the hands of those who did not understand it. Gert Biesta, in his fertile discussion of the weaknesses of education in our time, suggests that the most potent and forgotten forms of education are 'an act of creation ... bringing something new into the world, something that did not exist before'.[21] And creation itself can be understood as a beautiful risk, in the sense that God risks failure, not being in control of the materials, 'noise, dissent, resistance' – and God may have variant attitudes towards that risk.[22] The same risks pertain in creation and in teaching.

Placed within the frame of Jesus as Lord (the title Luke uses in his narration of the confrontation with the Pharisees and lawyers), the teacher becomes one who realizes that his teaching, itself a creative act, could and would go wrong in the same way as God's creation went wrong. Jesus comes into view as a teacher who would prefer the risk of being misinterpreted, having his words twisted, having the frustration of his learners' repeated failure, rather than the more straightforward method of forcing his understanding on people. Jesus as Lord, standing in the gap between the kingdom and the failure to understand it, is a radical thinker made of the same stuff as his hearers – an 'organic intellectual'[23] rather than a pedagogical *deus ex machina*. He resists the temptation to bring his followers 'some alien truth from above'.[24] The implications of his choice are enormous for him as teacher and saviour.

After the double question, do we detect any changes in Jesus' message or method, any indication that his introspection in the critical incident has prompted a new approach? The two parables, of the mustard seed and the woman's yeast, emphasize the kingdom's rapid and wide growth. The confrontations continue. The message of the kingdom, the counterpart of normal hierarchies, continues to become sharper. The predictions of Jerusalem and the passion become more frequent. The comments on cognitive failure all but disappear. They have been a recurrent feature up to this point, and have now been set aside. Was Jesus' critical incident the moment he realized his teaching would not, in itself, inaugurate the kingdom? That teaching and being misunderstood was a form of crucifixion? That it could lead to his actual death?

Jesus' message is a paradox between small-scale vulnerability and the exalted power and purposes of God. If Luke has an overriding theme to his portrait of Christ – a 'controlling Christology'[25] that centrally affects what he says about Jesus and what stories he chooses – it is probably the servanthood of Jesus in contrast with his post-resurrection exaltation. The attempt is to integrate the humiliation of the cross with the glory of the resurrection. The working out of this paradox, turning a contradiction into a resolution, is perhaps the ultimate purpose of Luke's writing,[26] and is what Luke the author means by his attempt at an 'orderly account ... that you may know the truth of the things of which you have been informed'.[27]

Conclusion

Luke's overriding Christological theme gives further potency to the moment of introspection. He may be showing us a teacher who, although he is Lord, remains puzzled by the paradox of his own kingdom, at times unable to communicate its vulnerability and its glory, at times powerless to break through the theological edifices of his culture with this new idea, and left wondering how he can describe it. As he struggled with his method, so also perhaps he struggled with the vast and strange idea that lies behind it. He would not be the first or last teacher to be puzzled by his content, to notice his hearers' failures, to interrogate his practice, or to realize that his knowledge changes, escapes and suffers.

Notes

1 Luke 13.18; Mark 4.30.
2 Luke 9.51ff.
3 Luke 10.21–24; 11.29–32; 12.54–56.
4 Luke 12.13–32.
5 Luke 11.37–54.
6 Luke 9.50; 11.23.
7 Luke 13.10–17.
8 Luke 13.1–5.
9 Luke 13.10–17.
10 Luke 13.6–9.
11 For example, Matthew 11.25.
12 Luke 11.52.
13 There may be other instances of Jesus wondering out loud, for example his question about whether it is lawful to do good or do harm on the sabbath (Luke 6.6–11), his question, 'Shall I come and heal him?' (the centurion's servant, Matthew 8.7) and his statement about feeding the children of Israel rather than giving food to dogs (Mark 7.24–30). Each case concerns a choice about observing Jewish purity laws or breaking them in the service of a higher good.
14 Jack Richards and Thomas Farrell, 2010, *Professional Development for Language Teachers*, Cambridge: Cambridge University Press, p. 13.
15 Khem Raj Joshi, 2018, 'Critical incidents for teacher professional development', *Journal of Nelta Surket* 5, online at www.nepjol.info/index.php/JNS/article/view/19493.
16 John Mason, 2002, *Researching your Own Practice: The discipline of noticing*, Abingdon and New York: Routledge.
17 Mason, 2002, p. xii.
18 Mason, 2002, p. 5.
19 David Tripp, 2012, *Critical Incidents in Teaching: Developing professional judgement*, Abingdon and New York: Routledge, p. xii.
20 Gert Biesta, 2016, *The Beautiful Risk of Education*, Abingdon and New York: Routledge.
21 Biesta, 2016, p. 11.
22 Biesta, 2016, pp. 14–15. See also John Caputo, 2006, *The Weakness of God: A theology of the event*, Indianapolis, IN: Indiana University Press.
23 Ted Newell, 2009, 'Worldviews in collision: Jesus as critical educator', *Journal of Education and Christian Belief* 13(2), pp. 141–54, p. 147.
24 Terry Eagleton, 1991, *Ideology: An introduction*, London: Verso, p. 119.

25 H. D. Buckwater, *The Character and Purpose of Luke's Christ-ology*, Cambridge: Cambridge University Press, 1996, p. 6.

26 Buckwater, 1996, p. 27.

27 Luke 1.3–4.

11

Now at last you are speaking clearly: John's Jesus as a teacher of light

Introduction: John's Gospel as memory

The text of John's Gospel is memory, but it interweaves two contrasting operative styles of memory: narration of incidents or conversations, and poetic discourses. The incidents and conversations are similar in style, brevity and urgency, though not so much in content, to the material in the synoptic Gospels. Whether the fourth Gospel was written before or after the synoptics, its narration takes much of the synoptic events as already known, and builds from them rather than repeating them. Events are told with a degree of detail that has led many to believe that the author was the beloved disciple, and was actually there.[1]

The discourses are long meditations quite unlike anything in the synoptic Gospels, placing into Jesus' mouth some poetic or hymnic passages that develop theological ideas about Christ's identity and the world's response. In comparison with the synoptics, John has more and deeper theology, and fewer events. The interleaving of narration and discourse is the creation of a post-resurrection community. That community, probably in Ephesus and perhaps also in Antioch, glorified Jesus as their teacher and Lord. Memory operates through both textual styles: in narration of events and insight into motives, refracted through memory of the resurrection; and in discourses ascribed to a spiritual teacher who spoke into their hearts. The first style is probably the direct recall of the beloved disciple, as mediated through scribes and editors;[2] the second is a form of call and response in which members of a community project their loving desire for their teacher into words they feel him speaking to them, words they receive as coming from him. This is clear from the way the discourses sometimes mix John's commentary into the purported words of Jesus – in the priestly prayer, for example, where the words 'and Jesus Christ whom you have sent' appear as part of the discourse,[3] and in the speech to Nicodemus, where the conversation is interrupted with 'God loved the world so much that he gave his only Son'.[4] The discourses are a fine blend of taught memory and commentary: it is probably impossible to distinguish the parts with certainty.

The Johannine community operated as a middle ear for followers remembering and longing for their spiritual teacher: it was the timpanic cavity holding and amplifying the sound of Jesus' voice, carrying it into the inner ear and the human mind.

Jesus, the beloved teacher

John's Gospel brings us Jesus as a teacher in community memory, both nearer to Jesus than the synoptics and yet more distant. It is a record authorized by one who actually knew the teacher intimately, and who left behind a theological meditation on him that was more coherent and unified than the synoptics; yet it seems more distant because it is overlaid with the community's spiritual discourses, some of them lengthy, intricate and paradoxical, about the status of Jesus as Christ.

John's Jesus is a teacher who belongs to John and his community. We cannot see beyond the interpretive curtain that John provides; we cannot see into Jesus' classroom; we can, however, see into John's, and through his mediation we gain a picture of Jesus. We approach John as the teacher speaking in old age about his own teacher. The memory held by John and his community – a memory that in the Gospel text is biographical, emotional, spiritual, sacramental and pedagogical – is itself an insight into the teacher.

John's Jesus is also the divine teacher, the one sent by the Father, who is gradually revealed in the course of the Gospel as one with the Father. John's prologue deals with the eternal pre-existing Word; its textual structure observes and imitates the step that the Word takes from outside the world to incarnation and involvement. The theological prologue opens with eternity, a world of light and life, a mystical state beyond;[5] from there it plunges the Word – and the reader – into this world, the world of John the Baptist;[6] and the third section mingles the Word with the World.[7] This is, in miniature, the point of John. Jesus is a teacher of light, coming from beyond.

The Gospel has been described as music, as the most divine of all divine books, and its author as divine; certainly its subject is a teacher held in the highest possible glorification and love.

A teacher within

By the time John presents Jesus to us, his subject has already been internalized as John's inner teacher. Jesus' first and last questions in the Gospel are significant pointers to this: 'What do you want?'[8] opens his first conversation with a future disciple; and 'Do you love me?'[9] indicates Jesus' intimacy with Peter at the end. For those who for textual reasons judge the Gospel to have concluded in Chapter 20, Jesus's final question is to Mary Magdalene: 'Who are you looking for?'[10] Each question is directed to an individual in the story, yet also carries with it the feeling that the reader is as much an interlocutor. The first question is an open-ended enquiry to a stranger; the last questions are intimate and loving. The progress from first to last is a journey that transforms the relationship with the teacher from neutrally cognitive to emotionally charged. By the end, John's teacher has invited and enfolded him into his heart, and into the heart of the divine.

There is less in John about place and more about person. The settings are existential rather than geographical or social. The synoptic habit of setting events in particular places, so that teaching is affected by context, is stripped away – which gives John's Gospel its intensely personal and universal mood.

John Hull, in his account of losing his sight and living with blindness, describes it as a 'fall ... out of consciousness, into the dreaming life, into the darkness. Later on ... the fall was discovered not to be out of consciousness, but into it. A new consciousness was born.'[11] When we turn from the highly visual, contextualized and eventful synoptics to the contrasting inwardness of John's Gospel, we are dealing with literature that is in some ways sightless and all the more insightful for it. John's Jesus speaks to the individual as if in a darkened room – relatively devoid of visual clues, immediate, direct. John's teacher teaches with an extraordinary personal intensity. Addressing suffering, he says, 'I have told you all this, so that when the time for it comes, you may remember that I told you.'[12]

The nature of this teacher is that he was the light who came into the world. Pre-existent, from the Father, shining in darkness and not overpowered by it,[13] the teacher is portrayed by John from the very start as both deeply personal within each hearer, yet also universal, addressing all through time and space. The personal teacher is the one who invites his hearer to 'make your home in me, as I make mine in you'.[14] The world's teacher is one who 'has come into this world'[15] for judgement, and who addresses the whole world by creating a sense of distance and difference: 'As long as I am in the world, I am the light of the world.'[16]

John alone of the four canonical Gospels omits the pericope of Jesus' question, 'Who do you say I am?' and Peter's confession of faith. It may be because John's Christology was more interested in Jesus as incarnate Word and Son of the Father than as Messiah; it may also be that John assumed the question to be unnecessary, since he was furnishing the richness of the answer. In a way, John's entire Gospel is an answer to Jesus' 'who am I' – an answer conducted in terms that send the existential question right back to the reader. Perhaps the twentieth-century theologian Karl Barth was thinking of John when he taught that God the creator, acting through his son Jesus the Word made flesh, achieves an existential change in us: 'Tell me how it stands with your Christology, and I shall tell you who you are.'[17] For the Benedictine scholar of eastern religions Lawrence Freeman, Jesus' question poses a challenge to every reader's identity and ego. Jesus, like many great gurus, teaches inwardly and outwardly: 'From the "exterior" he gives a push to the mind to turn inward: from the "interior" he pulls the mind toward the Self and helps in the quieting of the mind.'[18]

John's Gospel presents a teaching Jesus whose method includes questions shrouded in silence and stillness:

> The question of Jesus is significant because it touches the heart and wholeness of human experience, all our aspirations and deepest concerns. Listening to it can make us fully human. It simplifies us without the loss of human dignity.[19]

The teacher within has considerable existential power for individuals and the world.

A sign of contradiction

The influence of Gnosticism on John's Gospel may have many causative factors, and the degree of influence is still under discussion. There is the belief that the Johannine community was influenced by the 'introverted'[20] community of Qumran and its sectarian spirit of being apart from the world. There is also the evidence that Jesus, through John the Baptist, absorbed Gnostic ideas.[21] Johannine scholarship before the discovery of the Dead Sea scrolls placed scant emphasis on Gnosticism as a factor in Jesus' context, seeing it as something that entered Christianity later rather than predating it.[22] But it is clear that Gnosticism, in its multiple variant forms, had hallmarks that transferred themselves into the theology and practice of John's Jesus, including the central idea of the divine teacher who is ridiculed and humiliated but imparts special knowledge to his select followers before returning to heaven.[23] Whatever the sources or degree of the influence, John's teacher was one who divided and judged. John had Jesus dramatically entering a dark world from above, before returning to his father. 'If this is not gnosis, it is remarkably close.'[24]

It is also fair to note that John applied the Gnostic doctrine that forms of life in this world have a better, truer counterpart, seen only by the select few. He gave Jesus titles or identities accordingly: living water welling up to eternal life,[25] bread of life,[26] light of the world,[27] gate of the sheepfold,[28] good shepherd,[29] the way, the truth and the life,[30] true vine.[31] He implied that Jesus was, in effect, the true temple.[32] It is one thing for a teacher to be described as *a* good shepherd or *a* light, quite another to be described with the definite article, and with the word 'true', thus conferring an absolute status, surpassing or contradicting lesser goods. He is *the* light, in contrast to the lights lit in the temple where he was teaching; he is *the* bread of life, in contrast to the manna their forefathers had in the desert.

The consistent suggestion is that the everyday forms of religion, the ritual objects and stories, are matter, and he is spirit. Those who belong to this world, who hold matter to be good, know no better and find their value assumptions inverted: 'It is for judgement that I have come into this world, so that those without sight may see, and those with sight turn blind.'[33]

This true light, this ultimate teacher, nevertheless has to prove his worth in long and dramatic confrontations. One such passage interleaves a poetic discourse ascribed to Jesus with close narration of quarrelsome questioning.[34] Jesus' authority is once again in question when the Pharisees raise a legally reasonable objection that he has no independent testimony to his status as light of the world. Jesus acknowledges the validity of their objection, but says that he is above the law, 'because I know where I came from and where I am going; but you do not know …'.[35] Knowledge is another form of absolute division. The Gnostic idea that Jesus is from beyond this world, with all its compromises, was introduced in the prologue and is reintroduced in this quarrel, taking root as part of the spirit/matter, light/dark, knowledge/ignorance duality. In the middle of this passage comes the miraculous giving of sight to a man born blind. A clear implication, served up with tragic irony, is that the critics are spiritually blind. Their vanity, counter-suggestibility and wilfulness are made obvious in a detailed record of the dialogue. Their violence lies only just under the surface: 'You want to kill me because nothing I say has penetrated into you ... You want to kill me when I tell you the truth.'[36] Jesus divides light and dark, truth and falsehood, very sharply in this passage, with 'dramatically divisive'[37] apocalyptic language. He applies a classically Gnostic judgement: 'You are from below; I am from above. You are of this world; I am not of this world.'[38]

It is worth reminding ourselves that there are two forms of memory at work here. The teacher whose discourses are all about himself and his authority, his superiority, and his status above the law and the temple, is a teacher in John's long-term memory, a teacher John glorifies. From comparison with the synoptic Gospels, there is little doubt that Jesus' authority to teach and to heal was challenged in the temple and elsewhere. But the razor-sharp division between righteous and unrighteous, apparently applied by Jesus in this passage, removes any focus on the kingdom and instead makes Jesus himself the issue and the judge. As a portrait of a teacher this is less than attractive, unless we remember the function of John's memory and how it can project a moral ethos on to a departed beloved figure. That Jesus was an embattled teacher we know from all four Gospels. That he was also a vindicated teacher, decorated in memory with the distinction of having been light in darkness, is something we hear passionately from John. Jesus was a sign of contradiction. He forced moral choices.

A teacher who invites and attracts

There is another facet to John's memory of Jesus as teacher, one that emphasizes his spiritual power to invite and attract his learners. That Jesus always knows and sees more than his disciples is a recurrent theme – one noted by Kierkegaard, who links it to Jesus' divinity.[39] For example, Thomas wants to know where Jesus is going, and Philip wants to be shown the Father.[40]

There are several moments at which the harsh dualities of Gnosticism are eased away by a teaching approach that seems to encourage the possibility of making progress in the truth. The dualities are turned into pathways. The sense that the ignorant and blind must always be separate from the wise children of the light is softened by the possibility of change. Early examples of this are seen in Jesus' conversations with Nicodemus and with the woman at the well. John paints both these encounters in a contrast of light and dark. Nicodemus came to see Jesus by night; the woman was a Samaritan. Both encounters are instances of light prevailing over darkness, in fulfilment of John's prologue. Although Jesus is clear with Nicodemus that there is a difference between those born of flesh and those born of spirit, he is also clear that a second birth from above is possible.[41] And with the woman at the well, he promises that 'the hour is coming' when she and others can graduate from localized worship to universal worship in spirit and in truth – as different as well water is from the inner spring leading to eternal life.[42]

That one step in learning can lead on to another is repeatedly hinted at, in references to steps from knowledge to complete knowledge, from metaphor to plain speaking, from sowing to reaping, from hiddenness to glory. In the second farewell discourse, when Jesus teaches them about his Father's love for them,[43] 'the disciples find in this ... statement a clarity no longer masked in parable',[44] and so they declare their belief. Clarity leads on to clarity. It is even possible to detect a pattern in which learning leads at first to greater confusion before going on to clarity.[45]

The sense that the disciples make progress in their understanding of Jesus – that they have already made progress, and can make more – is returned to at several points in the discourse:

I still have many things to say to you, but they would be too much for you now, but when the Spirit of truth comes, he will lead you to the complete truth, since he will not be speaking for himself but will say only what he has learnt; and he will tell you of the things to come.[46]

It is interesting to note in passing here John's assumption that the Spirit also learns from the Father, as the Son does. This is the early raw material for what later became the doctrine of the Trinity. Here and in several other discourses we are invited into the life of the Trinity by a teacher who comes from above, full of grace and truth.

John also lets us have a sense that Jesus, the teacher within, can modify his teaching approach when he notices signs of progress or need, for example in whether or not to use metaphors.[47] The disciples are learners whose need is sometimes to be scolded or prompted ('How can you say, "Let us see the Father"? Do you not believe ...?'[48]), sometimes to be comforted ('There is no need to be afraid, little flock, for it has pleased your Father to give you the kingdom'[49]), sometimes encouraged, their progress recognized ('You are pruned already, by means of the word that I have spoken to you'[50]), and sometimes to be shown their next steps ('But when the Spirit of truth comes, he will lead you to the complete truth'[51]). Jesus meets all four of these needs in his learners. There is no discernible sense in the Gospel that their progress is linear, except perhaps at the very end.

In the service of progress in understanding, repetition of key words is used as a device for building up a concept gradually. The repetition of life and love are key to this strategy.[52]

The farewell discourse is preparation for the next steps, in which they will have to become less dependent on Jesus and carry their teacher within them in the form of the Spirit. He reassures them that he has confidence in their knowledge and their ability to find the way, and he emphasizes a relationship of love that can overcome the pain of parting.[53] He promotes them from servants to friends.[54]

Ultimately their unity with their teacher is assured. The themes of the glorification of the Son, the growing knowledge of his followers, their destiny having been taken from the world – 'they do not belong to the world any more than I belong to the world'[55] – and their belonging to their teacher and to the Father in unity, are all wrapped together in the priestly prayer.[56] As well as being a memory of eucharistic and eschatological power, in which Jesus has lifted his eyes to heaven, it is a kind of culmination to learning. If John's Gospel is a Gnostic-influenced text, it 'diverges from Gnosticism ... in its insistence upon the salvific will of God'.[57] Gnosticism is often a pessimistic strand of thought that divides people into followers of light or dark; but this is not where John's Jesus leaves his own. The harsh dualities of Gnostic thought cannot be erased from the picture of Jesus. They may exist in part to point up the positive by emphasizing negatives, a 'double-sided revelation';[58] the Gnostic strain and resemblance is still there. But John in the end, and after years of remembering and reflecting, shows us a teacher who makes sense to his followers, whose knowledge leads not to escape from the world but to salvation.[59] John's Jesus is more than 'an emissary of the heavenly world, as in Gnosticism',[60] and more than a revealer of God; he is God, offering his followers a path of learning in which he is both the explainer and the explained. His teaching is pictured as productive and fruitful more than it is judgemental.

Notes

1 The earliest tradition of John the disciple's authorship is from Irenaeus of Lyons in 180 CE. There is a discussion of the problems with this assumption in Oscar Cullmann, ET 1976, *The Johannine Circle*, London: SCM Press, pp. 63ff.

2 John 21.24.

3 John 17.3.

4 John 3.16.

5 John 1.1–5.

6 John 1.6–8.

7 John 1.9–14.

8 John 1.38.

9 John 21.15–17.

10 John 20.15.

11 John Hull, 1990, *On Sight and Insight: A journey into the world of blindness*, Oxford: Oneworld Publications, p. xiii.

12 John 16.4.

13 John 1.5–14.

14 John 15.4.

15 John 9.39.

16 John 9.5.

17 Karl Barth, ET 1949, *Dogmatics in Outline*, London: SCM Press, p. 66.

18 Lawrence Freeman, 2000, *Jesus: The teacher within*, New York and London: Continuum, p. 48, quoting the guru Ramana Maharshi.

19 Freeman, 2000, p. 52.

20 Philip Esler, 1994, *The First Christians in their Social Worlds: Social scientific approaches to New Testament interpretation*, London: Routledge, pp. 70ff.

21 Cullmann, 1976, pp. 57ff.

22 C. K. Barrett, 1967, *The Gospel According to St John: An introduction with commentary and notes on the Greek text*, London: SPCK.

23 Bernard Simon, 2017, *The Essence of the Gnostics*, London: Arcturus Publishing, p. 7.

24 John Ashton, 2007, *Understanding the Fourth Gospel*, Oxford: Oxford University Press, p. 521. See also C. H. Dodd, 1954, *The Interpretation of the Fourth Gospel*, Cambridge: Cambridge University Press.

25 John 4.14.

26 John 6.35.

27 John 8.12.

28 John 10.7.

29 John 10.11.

30 John 14.6.

31 John 15.1–3.

32 John 2.22.

33 John 9.39.

34 John 8.13—9.41.

35 John 8.14.

36 John 8.37–40.

37 Ashton, 2007, p. 521.

38 John 8.23.

39 Howard V. Hong and Edna H. Hong (eds), 1985, *Søren Kierkegaard: Philosophical fragments*, Princeton, NJ: Princeton University Press, p. 11.

40 John 14.5–8.

41 John 3.3–10.

42 John 4.13–21.

43 John 16.27.

44 William Loader, 2017, *Jesus in John's Gospel: Structure and issues in Johannine Christology*, Grand Rapids, MI: Eerdmans, p. 64.

45 John 7.33–34.

46 John 16.12–13.

47 John 16.25–29.
48 John 14.9–10.
49 Luke 12.32.
50 John 15.3.
51 John 16.13.
52 J. van der Watt, 2008, 'Johannine Style: Some initial remarks on the functional use of repetition in the Gospel of John', *In die Skriflig (In Luce Verbi)* 42(1), pp. 75–99.
53 John 14.2–28.
54 John 15.15.
55 John 17.14.
56 John 17.1–26.
57 Ashton, 2007, p. 522.
58 Loader, 2017, p. 4.
59 Ruth Edwards, 2014, *Discovering John: Context, interpretation, reception*, London: SPCK, p. 68.
60 Loader, 2017, p. 4.

PART 3

How our hearts burned within us

The argument so far

The Gospel texts have suppressed themes, unresolved tensions and loose ends related to Jesus as a teacher. A conventional reading of the pedagogical passages in the Gospels gives only a limited understanding of his teaching role. By looking again at the texts with a teacher's eyes, we can discover new insights, which so far could be summarized as follows.

- The risen Christ encountered by his disciples is a mysterious and variable figure. The accounts of him play with semblance and reality, longing and transformation.
- He knew the content of the Torah and the prophets well, quoting from them with facility, but was impatient with those who failed to read the grand narrative of God's power, or who micro-interpreted Scripture to keep themselves or others in dependency.
- He was a teacher not only of ethics but also of hermeneutics and theological method, influenced by a wisdom-oriented reading of the law and the prophets. He taught a revolution in hermeneutics and wanted to instigate new interpretive practices in communities. He confronted the intellectual guardians whose power limited people's theological thinking. In his teaching, content, method and source were integrated.
- As an eschatological teacher, Jesus brought crisis to every classroom. All sites of learning were judged and came to destruction. No classroom, no structure, no organization could contain or manage him.

- He was a puzzling teacher even to those who showed him goodwill. His teaching was not always successful, consistent or admirable. Even when we account for the preoccupation of his followers with issues of insider and outsider status, we are still left with a teacher whose example cannot be held up as perfect. He was a teacher who developed, changed and had bad days.
- As a learning teacher, Jesus struggled with method and purpose. He was at times baffled by the immobility of theological ideas in people's minds and how to shift them, and was seeking his way on the purpose of his teaching and where it would lead.
- He was a teacher who inspired the deepest love. He invited and attracted his learners into light and love, drawing them forward into ever deeper revelation and knowledge.

The layered and puzzling nature of his teaching persona is intuitively caught by Elizabeth Templeton:

> He was cavalier about standards of knowledge. He didn't apparently know the difference between decency and indecency, given the people he affirmed. He didn't much classify, except between those who were willing to be involved out of their depth in the future of God, and those who would maintain their moral or religious intactness. He didn't know that you have to come to terms with the world as it is, and constantly proposed images of an alternative world ... What became of him is another story, with many variants, but some think that he made concrete the reversal of the Fall, showed how the limited flesh, with its tiredness and perishability, if it gives itself into the sufficient love which is God, may become a new thing, able to clap its hands and sing even through the sharpness of death.[1]

The normative reading of the Gospels conceals much about Jesus as a teacher. Ideological, social and cultural aspects of the text and context hide his teaching mind from us. What we have discovered in Part 2 still leaves many questions unanswered. In search of him as a teacher, we may have reached the limits of what can be known by conventional historical-critical methods. The inbreaking extravagance of God's kingdom is also a hallmark of Jesus' teaching approach: he was wildly compassionate, inconsistent, irresponsible, careless about his learners, unobservant of boundaries, yet profoundly loving. In his hands, meaning and understanding appear, disappear and reappear. The manner of his teaching invites his followers to deploy their imagination in creating him as a teacher.

For a teacher today reading the Gospels, three forces are at work, engaging their professional imagination in extending the text. The ambiguity and incompleteness of the Gospel texts on Jesus as teacher *necessitate* our use of imagination; the potency of Jesus as teacher *invites* our imagination; the content of revelation – Christ and his kingdom, his spirit with us – *create and recreate* our imagination.

Christian educators can give themselves permission to imagine and recover the teacher who has been lost or suppressed in the Gospel and tradition. They can use their own experience to bring to light stories of Jesus learning and encountering learners, and developing his self-awareness. Christian educators, if they have metaphorically been on the road with the learning and teaching Jesus, if they have sat down with him to break bread, will recognize him, imagine him, and know how he burns in their hearts, burns in their own thinking and feeling about their work. The pedagogical generosity of God is waiting to be imaginatively explored through a playful development of some Gospel themes.

'We must get rid of the idea that the one who teaches is superior to the one who learns.'[2] So Hull warns against the negative notion of learning and the effect it can have on our attitude to Christ. Linking learning to love, to creativity and to time, Hull reaches the conclusion that God can learn. God changes, 'from light to light, from beauty to beauty ... from knowledge to more knowledge'.[3] We might say that God learns from being in relationship with humanity and creation. 'To be omniscient is not to know everything but only to know everything which is available to be known.'[4] For example, it is not within the scope of omniscience to know what a baby's name will be when the name has not been chosen.

The Gospel text takes us so far; Christian educational imagination can also play a part. In Part 3, three chapters offer creative approaches to a further journey. These chapters challenge conventional readings of Jesus as a teacher with new pedagogical and Christological insights. They seek to apply the new insights in the Christian pedagogical imagination, intuiting stories about him (Chapter 12), exploring sacramental dimensions of teaching (Chapter 13), and considering the implications for the Trinity and the church (Chapter 14). It is hoped that these chapters might point to how Christian teachers can base their professional understanding on their faith in Christ, and how the churches might respond.

Notes

1 Elizabeth Templeton, 1977, 'You cannot know what you do not love', in Alastair Hulbert and Peter Matheson (eds), 2019, *In Your Loving is Your Knowing: Elizabeth Templeton: Prophet of our times*, Edinburgh: Birlinn Ltd, pp. 216–21, p. 219.

2 John Hull, 1985, *What Prevents Christian Adults from Learning?*, London: SCM Press, p. 236.

3 Hull, 1985, p. 226.

4 Hull, 1985, p. 232.

12

Writing an educational Christ

Introduction

In search of an authentic way of understanding J. S. Bach, the biographer Paul Elie poses the problem of authenticity thus: that Bach is thought to be the greatest keyboardist who ever lived, yet none of us has ever heard him play.[1] We may have heard his music and been deeply moved by it, but if we imagine that the sound we hear now is what Bach intended, we deceive ourselves. Indeed if we imagine that Bach's intentions were clear at the time, either to his colleagues and clients or even to himself, we deceive ourselves the more. The difficult reality is that Bach, an accomplished composer, 'a technician of the sacred',[2] cannot now be uncovered by any scholarly route of investigation of sources. Bach was an inventor and can best be discovered through invention. The search for authenticity takes Elie into 'a series of variations about inventions ... deliberately or intuitively worked out' by other musicians whose encounter with Bach brought them to unexpected places and new insights on both technique and transcendence.[3]

In Part 2 we saw how the biblical text, looked at with a teacher's eye, can reveal some new insights about Jesus the teacher; but it still leaves many questions unanswered. In this chapter we turn to the Christian pedagogical imagination to provide further insights, albeit of a very different sort: intuitive inventions, not scholarly discoveries, and experiments with variation rather than conventional theological methods. We delve into some adaptations of stories, and draw provisional conclusions about how the Christian pedagogical imagination might or might not work.

Challenging the power of conventional theology

We are going to take away from conventional theologians their monopoly over the discourse on Jesus as teacher. There are two specific manifestations of conventional power that have impacted badly on our understanding of Jesus as a teacher: first, the power to curb the Christian pedagogical imagination by determining what is and is not legitimate interpretation; second, the power to cover Jesus' shortcomings as a teacher by rationalizing or harmonizing his teaching as part of an all-knowing, pre-ordained divine schema.

Many authors have attempted to write Christ contextually so that he affirms the experience of oppressed groups. Douglas's black Christ[4] and Ragno's black Jesus[5] are portraits with reference to sources and key figures in the American civil rights and black power movements. Asian theologians speak of encountering Christ in 'the Jordan of Asian religion' and 'the Calvary of Asian poverty'.[6] For them, the structure of salvation is fully embedded within Asian culture and circumstances. Sarah Bessey,[7] Elisabeth Schüssler Fiorenza[8] and Cynthia Bourgeault,[9] among others, have explored Jesus and Christology in feminist frames, moving in and beyond the perceived rules of biblical hermeneutics. The editors of the *Queer Bible Commentary*[10] and Nancy Wilson's work on queer theology[11] create a similar framework for sexual minorities, adopting the term 'queer' to build a theology based on the experiences of lesbian, gay, bisexual and transgendered people.

What these hermeneutic rebels have in common is that they do not apologize for their experience, nor do they plead for their place; rather they affirm their lives as a place in which God chooses to be. They assume that in official hermeneutics the whole story has not been told, and then they develop a 'hermeneutics of remembrance or reclamation'[12] in order to detect unheard voices. While teachers as a group are not oppressed or marginalized, it can be said that the complexity of their craft has been forgotten or set aside in the text of the Gospels, and in much conventional preaching. For this reason, a methodology that imitates the liberation theologies employed by oppressed groups can be appropriate. And since Christian teachers are so often in the front line of mission, we should understand their experience rather than silence it.

Liberation theologies, in their various forms, have begun to suggest that churches and mainstream ways of doing theology are not capable of moving beyond their mindsets, particularly patriarchy, because they lack the intellectual fertility to imagine a hermeneutics based on marginal experience.[13] Official Christologies, in neglecting Christ's identification with marginalized groups, have forfeited their authenticity and orthodoxy. In the context of black theology – and the principle could be applied to other groups equally well – James Cone asserts that there is no relevance or productiveness in arguments that Jesus historically was not black. The literal colour of Jesus is held to be insignificant when compared with the point that he was definitely not white, either literally or culturally.[14] The spiritual and political readout from this is a Christian writing of Jesus the Christ as black, with revelation as blackness, human self-awareness as black and salvation history being synonymous with black experience.[15] In similar ways, writers have given themselves permission to speak of a Christ who is incarnate in their communal experience.

Leonardo Boff speaks of the church's permission and duty to develop a living discourse of Christ in people's own power contexts, but this need not tip a church over into any narcissistic stance in which its own immediate realities come to dominate and distort its vision of Christ:

> We can only speak with him as starting point, as persons touched by the significance of his reality. We come to him with that which we are and have, inserted into an unavoidable socio-historical context. We see with our own eyes the figure of Christ and reread the sacred texts that speak of him ...[16]

In rereading the sacred texts, some theologians break the restraints altogether with an explicit agenda of disrupting official hermeneutics. Distinctive among such writers is Marcella

Althaus-Reid, whose way of writing theology sets out deliberately to shock – 'doing theology without using underwear'[17] was her metaphor for upsetting the 'artificial, mannered and ostentatious ... righteousness'[18] of official theology. Her approach refuses to attempt respectability (in morals or in hermeneutics) as defined by western patriarchy.

The power to determine what is and is not a legitimate hermeneutics has become concentrated in patriarchal hands. Jesus the hermeneutic revolutionary has been shaped by patriarchy, and 'has become a monopoly with strict control on spiritual production of meaning and exchange'.[19] So we must ask where the knowledge of Christ comes from and who has previously had the authority to create this knowledge, stamp it with orthodoxy and disseminate it. Indecent theology 'has to raise doubts'[20] and has to 'produce a rupture in imaginative identifications'[21] of the patriarchal Christ, deconstructing in order to reconstruct, stripping in order to clothe.

Patriarchy is of particular salience to our search for the learning teacher who was Jesus. Patriarchy has disguised him as an omniscient teacher and created hierarchies of those around him, all of them to varying degrees passive, all in knowledge deficit. It has placed a premium on his knowing, and a taboo on his learning. In doing so, patriarchy has hidden the learning half of the teacher that we began to glimpse in Part 2 from the eyes of the church. 'Jesus was constructed in a way such that he was born to speak and to be silent at the same time.'[22]

Unlearning what we know

The task of writing an educational Christ must begin with unlearning what we think we know of Christ as teacher in order to construct him again as a learner-teacher. Educator-theologians can give ourselves permission to imagine and recover what has been lost or suppressed in the Gospel and tradition, bringing to light those stories of Jesus and his saints learning and encountering learners, and drawing out their full implications. Likewise, we can authoritatively identify places where Jesus the learning teacher got it wrong, as any learning teacher will from time to time, and we can expose the ways in which theology rushes ahead to the empty tomb in order to hide his mistakes and justify everything that he said and did. We raise these themes not to create another Jesus who conveniently reflects back to us our own educational predilections. A disruptive educational Christology cannot be a collective act of professional narcissism. We do it to add power to the question, 'Who is Jesus?' and to avoid the category errors and deceptions of crude translation into our time. We will discover a Jesus who challenges us as educators at least as much as he brings us comfort; he does this for everyone else (apart from the official theologians, who have tamed him so that he brings them only comfort and convenience), so we can live with confident hope that he will do it for us too. The way to bring such a Jesus to light is to use our imagination to enter the internal logic of some Gospel encounters, placing them alongside our own professional experiences.

By what authority (as they used to say in Galilee) do we conduct theology in this way? The legitimacy of writing freely about an educational Christ lies partly in what we already know of his own freedom in discourse. For example, we have a Christ who took risks with humour, pastiche and exaggeration: he gave ironical nicknames to his followers, such as Sons of Thunder;[23] he told stories whose plots took ridiculous and hyperbolic scale, such as the camel and the eye of the needle;[24] and he dished out satirical one-liners aimed at those in authority.[25] His parable of the leaven in the flour[26] is, to put it mildly, distant in style from respectable theology; it has been described as exaggerated, holding opposites together to the point of absurdity, highlighting the powerless people, dabbling with the unclean, and apparent nonsense.[27] Jesus was given to extravagance and liberality of speech, willing to communicate with a twist, preferring the risks of misunderstanding and offence over the security of direct messages.

Writers and film directors beyond number have sought to incarnate his unrestrained discourse in their own cultures, at the same time striving to explain or resolve the fault lines in the original plot. The multiple printed and celluloid incarnations cause Jesus to be 'perpetually reborn'[28] in successive cultures, each birth being an imaginative reshaping of an elusive original.

The pedagogic and Christian imagination

The creativity necessary for writing an educational Christ travels beyond obvious resemblances. The writer might be tempted, for example, to adapt narratives already given in the Gospels so that they are contextualized more obviously in a contemporary educational setting: the impact of his teaching, the call to follow him, the betrayal of a heroic charismatic teacher. These and other examples can be considered and rejected as mere mechanical translation, essentially deceptive because they are limited as flights of imagination.

The project to write an educational Christ can be characterized by playful originality, trust in professional experience, profound theological fidelity, and stylistic consistency. In keeping with reception approaches it is the purpose to maintain fidelity not to the text but to what lies behind the text, half-hidden. It is important to retain some consistency with the style of discourse because of its clearly political pointedness.

'As soon as we die, we enter into fiction.'[29] Hilary Mantel, writer of historical fiction, uses the example of a deceased family member remembered differently by relatives to make the point that fiction can convey truth. The three fictional short stories on Jesus that follow below are used in order to explore intuitively how the teacher might be for us. Two stories take well-known Gospel encounters and try to imagine the interior pedagogical structure of them; the third is an amalgam of Gospel incidents woven together to create what might have been thought and said. These stories are the subcutaneous muscle structure of the thinking about explanation and learning that might have gone on, unrecorded in the Gospels. They come from a Christian pedagogical imagination. One could accept or refute the claim that they expose what might have happened, or what might have been suppressed in the

Gospel text. But their main function is to release the teaching and learning Christ from the constraining power of conventional hermeneutics, and at the same time to free the Christian pedagogical imagination. Two birds take flight from their enclosures, and soar simultaneously.

The authorities try to test Jesus

This short story is an adaptation of a pericope narrating how a trick question is laid for Jesus by some Pharisees and Herodians.[30] As discussed in Chapter 4, this incident may be a reflection of early church conflicts over their relationship with Judaism. But its status and common usage in contemporary preaching and teaching has inserted it into the church's consciousness as a hallmark of Jesus' teaching. How might it seem if appropriated by teachers?

Some senior leaders and inspectors came to Jesus with a question that they hoped would catch him out and enable them to condemn him for lowering standards. 'Jesus,' they said to him, 'by all the reports, you are an inspired teacher and your staff development sessions are a wow. You have said, and we quote from eye witnesses, "The learning I'm looking for is not to be found in the formal measures of pupil progress; the happiest and most real learners are the ones who ponder deeply and say nothing; they really value their learning. You claim that spiritual and moral development are at the heart of your school; I say to you that measurement and judgement are at the heart of your school." So tell us, Jesus, there are so many teachers who struggle with this: how did we get to the state where we value what is measurable, rather than doing what we should, which is to measure what is valuable?'

Jesus looked at them and saw they were trying to catch him out. He quickly ran through the possible answers in his mind: all of them were dangerous. To say what many of his followers believed – that the data business in schools is useless, oppressive and a distraction – would provoke accusations that he did not care about high standards or lifting young people out of poverty, and that he was willing to dumb down. To say the opposite – that measurements of progress are important and we must focus relentlessly on them – was just the same old discourse. To say that he recognized the problem but didn't have a solution would look feeble or evasive. To tell his questioners where to get off, with their slippery trick questions and fake humility, would be to lose the moral high ground.

Above all, what Jesus wanted to say was something that would turn the question back on them, while at the same time giving his educational colleagues hope; something that would render the problem less huge, less worrying; something that would make his questioners look a little bit silly for asking, but stop short of humiliating them.

All this went through Jesus' mind in less than a minute. He said, 'Bring me your school data summary.'[31] They showed him one. 'What data do you see here? What is this information all about?' They answered, 'You know as well as we do. It is a statistical measurement of the progress being made by the learners in literacy and numeracy, and their attendance. Our question is: does all this measurement add up to anything valuable, yes or no?' And Jesus handed them back the document. 'Well then,' he said, 'measure what is measurable, and value what is valuable.' And they were astonished.

This version ends with exactly the sense of satisfaction seen in its Gospel original: Jesus 2, Pharisees 0. But we have to bear in mind that this kind of 'win' shows Jesus in the best light from the vantage point of a post-resurrection community convinced that he should be vindicated in every way. We should also note that Jesus' answer is, essentially, a fudge. It does not answer their question; it is more a rebuttal than a reply. The constraining factors operating on Jesus the teacher have not been lifted, they have merely migrated from one context to another. Jesus is still, as it were, caught in the crossed searchlights of false binaries.

Jesus learns that he needs to change his teaching priorities

Jesus' encounter with the Syro-Phoenician woman[32] is a key battleground in hermeneutics. The woman and her daughter are doubly outsiders, doubly discriminated against by race and gender. That a woman's voice is heard at all is 'extraordinary ... and functions deconstructively to subvert the androcentrism of the text'[33] – and more so since she actually argues with Jesus, overcoming his three refusals. The story appears in all three synoptic Gospels; Matthew, with his concern for ritual purity and the boundaries between clean and unclean, might well have left it out, so its inclusion there gives it extra weight. Historical or not, the incident is told with such psychological vividness that it draws us in, and endows the woman with significant attributes: her ethnicity, her gender, the urgency of her need, the quick-wittedness and defiance of her speech, all highlighted for our perception and reaction.[34] She is a gendered, embodied interlocutor in a form of theological literature that treats women's bodies with disdain when it thinks about them at all, and in a world where women were vulnerable.[35]

It happened that Jesus was teaching in the coastal area, in a town where extremes of wealth and poverty lived side by side. The authorities had dumped many refugee families there, leaving them with no community support, no language training, no citizenship programmes and no help for the women. There had been a middle-class flight from the local schools into independent providers, leaving the maintained schools, including the one where Jesus worked, to clean up the mess if they could. Jesus found it a desperate and depressing place; he was doing supply and wanted to get out and move on as soon as possible.

One day at the end of school, a girl in Year 10 stayed behind, accompanied by her mate and sidekick, both of them scrawny and sickly-looking mixed-race girls, perhaps from Syria, whose names Jesus did not even know. His heart sank when he saw them: he was tired, ragged and had a headache.

The first girl complained aggressively that neither she nor her friend could understand his lessons. Pointing to her sidekick, she mouthed the word 'Epilepsy.' Jesus retorted that they should try harder to keep up, and anyway he had a meeting to attend. But the girl wouldn't stop. He said in reply, 'If you people are not interested in my lessons, there's nothing I can do for you.' The girl then astonished and embarrassed Jesus by making an extreme gesture of supplication, which he supposed was a custom in her culture. 'Sir! HELP US!' He replied, 'If I teach to the slowest pace in the class, the others will get restless. I'm here to help the ones who have real potential.' And her reply was, 'Yes, sir, but don't you think we've all got potential?' Then Jesus decided to miss his meeting, and sat down with both of them to give them extra help. And their progress improved from that day on.

Too easy, isn't it? Too happy an ending. It leaves unsolved the mystery of why a supposedly good and divine teacher would be so heartless to a learner in need, casually dishing out a racial and sexual slur. Conventional preaching suggests this was a test of her faith; to any teacher, a lame explanation. Also unexplored are the questions of why he did not similarly reject approaches from others, what he would have done if she had given up, and why his willingness to help should depend on her answers. It seems more likely that Jesus' own prejudices are challenged by this nameless girl, goading him into some kind of reconsideration of his priorities – a potent case of the learning teacher, 'an initially sexist, but finally teachable man'.[36] The realities of Jesus' life, and of teachers' lives now, make that kind of encounter rare. The costs of responding positively are quite high in lost prestige, and the signs of pedagogical success come slowly and ambiguously. The miraculous outcome of the biblical story fails on all counts to grapple with these realities. An alternative ending might be:

Jesus refused, and walked out. Afterwards, he deeply regretted his lack of compassion, and went to find them, to offer them some special help. To his shame he saw that they had already left the building. The following day, they were marked absent. The next time Jesus saw them, he felt a little more sympathetic, but still he did not know what he could do.

We leave this story with Jesus' problem unsolved. We can speculate on his options, but we cannot live inside the comfortable assumption that he effected a miracle here as apparently he did at Tyre and Sidon. Years later, when his friends were telling stories and swapping examples of his teaching, they might have wondered why this episode had no ending. What should a good teacher do, when the example of Jesus the educator is incomplete? Did he release the nameless girls from their poverty trap? Did he take them with him when he moved on? Did he go to the authorities about them? Did they take the situation into their own hands? It may be that Jesus' friends decided on the most satisfying outcome, and propagated it not because it happened but because it should have happened, they wanted it to happen, and it was consistent with the known part of the story.

If we were to write the next pericope, at the end of school on the following day, what do we think would occur? What do we want to happen? What intervention by Jesus will change life for these girls? How will any intervention, which could be a 'miracle', be written and told of? What does this tell us about anything that has been emphasized in the Gospel narrative, and what does it suggest has been suppressed? What does it show us about our need for stories of deprivation to have happy endings?

Hurrying into the hill country: Mary as Jesus' first teacher

The hill country was where Mary went to be with her pregnant cousin Elizabeth.[37] It was where these two women learnt to be theologians of God's coming reign of justice. There they exchanged their dramatic news; one or both of them sang words that we now know as the Magnificat;[38] they crafted a theology by women, a theology that upended the normative patriarchy of the Torah. Their obedience was to the promises of God, not to any man, religious rule, culture or creed. We can better understand Jesus the teacher when we imagine how being Mary's son shaped his theology, his knowledge and use of the Torah; and this realization helps us in 'ending the captivity of Christ in kyriarchal biblical systems'.[39] Kyriarchal systems are structures of theology and hermeneutics that privilege male and elite frames of reference. Far from being the personification of subjection – the impossible ideal of virgin mother that the church has made her – what if Mary was a woman of deep power, the second Miriam, prophetess and singer of her people's liberation?[40]

The hill country is not a synagogue or temple, not a town or a monastic community. It is a deliberately vague hinterland, a place for marginalized discourse; a space for their imagination to dip deep into the tradition and discover its radicalism for themselves, because it was not on offer to them in any mainstream place belonging to Judaism.

Jesus often used to talk about his mother. He pointed to Miriam as the reason why he became a teacher. The Magnificat, her song of praise for an intervening, righteous God, demonstrates a knowledge of Jewish Scripture and a passionate trust in God's capacity to overthrow injustice – qualities she passed on to her son.

Miriam took the song from her forebear, Hannah, mother of the prophet Samuel.[41] Hannah's song of an exultant heart praising the power and holiness of God, disrupting the arrogant and mighty, became Miriam's own. She sang it to Jesus in the womb, she sang it to him on her knee, she sang it to coax him to sleep and calm him, she sang it on the way to synagogue to tune up his spiritual senses. 'What God has done,' Jesus used to say, 'is what God will do: look, how he has pulled down the mighty ... he has lifted up the lowly ... he has shown strength with his arm ... he has scattered the proud in the imagination of their hearts ... my mother taught me in the song that our past gives us hope for our future ... our memory is our kingdom. She sang it, so I had to teach it!'

In the Magnificat we hear not only the voice of Hannah but the questioning of a young girl. Perhaps the words were Elizabeth's before they were Miriam's – the reference to barrenness fits her condition neatly. Elizabeth asked the angel, 'How shall I know this?' Miriam asked, 'How shall this happen?' Her visitant told her not to be afraid; from then on, she never let fear deter her from questioning. Miriam interpreted visions and texts. She took the initiative. They were women who required an explanation. They were women who would not take the authoritative male word unless it came with a convincing reason.

Miriam's questioning spirit, alive in her son, drove him to go and look for a truer Judaism elsewhere, beyond the home, beyond the synagogue. 'How is it that you cannot read the signs of the times?' Jesus asked. 'If salt loses its taste, how can it be seasoned again? What woman would not light a lamp, sweep the house, and search thoroughly?' and, at the end, 'Why have you forsaken me?' Jesus learnt to ask questions of authority figures from his fearless, questioning, remembering mother.

The words of Miriam's song are studded with prophetic insight, much of it from Isaiah and Ezekiel, and with quotations from the Psalms. When Jesus reads from the scroll in his home town, he is reading again about what God has done – 'he has anointed me' – from the same chapter in Isaiah that Miriam's song quotes from.[42] We can imagine him learning the Torah and the prophets with her, the two of them sitting together at the scroll open at Isaiah chapter 61, reading alternate verses. The spirit of the Lord Yahweh has been given to me! Jesus recites. (Yes, thinks Miriam, that is even truer than you might know now.) I exult for joy in Yahweh, Miriam intones, my soul rejoices in my God, for he has clothed me in the garments of salvation ... like a bridegroom ... (And Jesus, listening and watching, wonders why there is always a smile of memory on her face when she reaches that point in the text.)

If they read to the end of that chapter, they see God's promise is that integrity and praise will spring up in the sight of the nations, just as a garden makes seeds spring up.[43] The high drama of the prophetic vision of the kingdom was common to mother and son. And again, as with his mother, what is called up from the holy past of Israel is then intensified into an eschatological present. Miriam must have been a teacher of extraordinary intensity, one who enthralled her listening son with her knowledge and love of the Torah, her sense of its immediate and dramatic possibility.

'Who is my mother?'[44] he later quipped, in a moment that has sometimes struck a chill note, as if it were an act of rejection against her. We so often assume that Miriam at that moment represents domesticity and docility, quiet conformist piety, a set of values that Jesus is determined to reject. But what if her son is at that moment seeking to share with the crowd everything his mother has given him – her fluency with the prophets, her dramatic and intelligent trust in God? What if he is asking, 'Who can be like my mother? Anyone who does the will of my father can live up to the example of my mother.'

Later, Luke narrates the voice of an anonymous woman in the crowd: 'Happy the womb that bore you and the breasts you sucked!'[45] It is a wonderfully physical blessing, full of gutsy embodied spontaneity; it is easy to imagine Matthew and John, pens ready to scratch out anything impure, suppressing such words; and indeed the incident appears nowhere else in the Gospels. Did Jesus remember then that his mother had sung how all generations would call her blessed? Did he, in framing his reply – 'Still happier are those

who hear the word of God and keep it!' – think of his mother
in those terms, as a prophet who had heard God's word, kept
it, and inspired him with its power? Jesus does not belittle his
mother in these passages; he elevates her as his prime source
of divine intuitive wisdom and his first example of radical
obedience to divine righteousness.

The mother of Christ formed for us, in her womb, on her
knee, a teacher – and to do this she too must have been a
teacher. She taught him salvation history and radical, present-
moment trust in God's promises. She was full of grace and
truth. 'The living remembrance of this woman can ... inspire
the struggle for God's compassionate and liberating justice.'[46]

This is more of an experimental variation than the previous
two stories. It explores the human backstory to Jesus' becoming a teacher. We know nothing of Mary's literacy, but the
story intuits that she passed on her knowledge and love of the
Torah and the prophets to her son, and with it her immersion
in wisdom. There are icons that depict her teaching Jesus to
read. It is unlikely that her theological knowledge could have
been seen as normal; but what normal family could have produced a teacher such as Jesus? Remembrance of this sort can
be neither verified nor falsified. But things could have been this
way.

What became of Mary after the loss of her son? She was
there, she saw the full outpouring of human cruelty. Did she
ever recover from the memories? Did the followers of the
way look after her? Could any form of familial or communal
normality hold her after all that? 'I do not go the synagogue
now,' says Mary to herself in old age. 'All of that is gone. I
would be noticed; my strangeness would stand out.'[47] How
does the church look after her now? Do we believe her, or
have we silenced her?

Conclusion

These three stories are experiments in intuition and variation. They mark stages in stylistic development, stages in setting us free from the power of conventional theologies. The Christian pedagogical imagination can be released, but it will not fly from its enclosure if we seek, in telling our own stories, only to imitate the happy endings and successful outcomes of the constructed Jesus presented in the official Gospels. In the great pedagogical generosity of God, the gatekeepers of rigour and control have been flouted, but the struggle is bloody. In the pedagogy of the kingdom, rigour does not have to mean control, obedience does not have to mean submission, and compassion does not inevitably lead to disorder. Stories of Jesus the teacher help us to dream of an end of the dualities.

The telling of such stories celebrates Jesus as the one in whom all our educational conflicts are represented and dramatized: binaries vs integrity; authority vs chaos; knowledge vs skills and attitudes; achievement vs reflection; status vs equality; purity and accuracy vs trangressive creativity and self-expression; love of learners as erotic vs platonic; failure vs success. He is the one on whom all the educational pathologies that derive from our inability to resolve these conflicts are laid, are projected. In this sense, Jesus is the one who shows us ourselves, just as Barth said.[48]

Notes

1 P. Elie, 2013, *Reinventing Bach*, London: Union Books, p. 4.

2 Elie, 2013, p. 6.

3 Elie, 2013. p. 7.

4 Kelly Brown Douglas, 2019, *The Black Christ*, 25th anniversary edn, Maryknoll, NY: Orbis Books.

5 Stephen Ragno, 2011, *Black Jesus in the Twentieth Century*, New York: Lambert Academic Publishing.

6 A. Pieris, *An Asian Theology of Liberation*, Maryknoll, New York: Orbis Books, 1988, p. 63.

7 Sarah Bessey, 2013, *Jesus Feminist: God's radical notion that women are people too*, London: Darton, Longman and Todd.

8 Elisabeth Schüssler Fiorenza, 1994, *Jesus: Miriam's Child, Sophia's Prophet: Critical issues in feminist Christology*, New York: Continuum.

9 Cynthia Bourgeault, 2008, *The Wisdom Jesus: transforming heart and mind*, Boston, MA: Shambhala Publications.

10 D. Guest, R. Goss, M. West and T. Bohache (eds), 2006, *The Queer Bible Commentary*, London: SCM Press.

11 Nancy Wilson, 2000, *Our Tribe: Queer folks, God, Jesus and the bible*, San Francisco, CA: Alamo Square Distributors.

12 Thomas Bohache, 2006, 'Matthew', in Guest, Goss, West and Bohache (eds), pp. 487–516, p. 488.

13 Sandra M. Schneiders, 2004, *Beyond Patching: Faith and feminism in the Catholic Church*, Mahwah, NJ: Paulist Press.

14 A. Hennelly, 1995, *Liberation Theologies: The global pursuit of justice*, Mystic, CT: Twenty-third Publications, pp. 101–2.

15 Hennelly, 1995, p. 120.

16 Leonardo Boff, 1978, *Jesus Christ Liberator: A critical Christology for our time*, Maryknoll, New York: Orbis Books, p. 43.

17 Marcella Althaus-Reid, 2000, *Indecent Theology: Theological perversions in sex, gender and politics*, London: Routledge, p. 11.

18 Althaus-Reid, 2000, p. 100.

19 Althaus-Reid, 2000, p. 95.

20 Althaus-Reid, 2000, p. 96.

21 Althaus-Reid, 2000, p. 99.

22 Althaus-Reid, 2000, p. 107.

23 Mark 3.16–17.

24 Matthew 19.24.

25 Matthew 23.24.

26 Luke 13.21.

27 P. Lampe, 2012, *Theology in a Secular World*, London: T&T Clark, pp. 125ff.

28 A. Reinhartz, 2007, *Jesus of Hollywood*, Oxford: Oxford University Press, p. 20.

29 Hilary Mantel, 2017, 'The day is for the living', First BBC Reith Lecture, 13 June 2017, online at www.bbc.co.uk/programmes/p055sv69 (accessed 25/06/17).

30 Luke 20.20–26. There are slightly abbreviated parallels in Matthew 22.15–22 and Mark 12.13–17.

31 At the time of writing, the 'school inspection data summary report' is the UK government's instrument for schools to present and interpret their data on pupil progress in the curriculum. It is used in school improvement and in inspections.

32 Matthew 15.21–28.

33 Elaine Wainwright, 1994, 'The Gospel of Matthew', in Elisabeth Schüssler Fiorenza (ed.), *Searching the Scriptures: A feminist commentary*, New York: Crossroad Publishing, pp. 635–77, pp. 651–2.

34 Amy-Jill Levine with Marianne Blickenstaff (eds), 2001, *A Feminist Companion to Mark*, Sheffield: Sheffield Academic Press, p. 96.

35 Alan Cadwallader, 2008, *Beyond the Word of a Woman: Recovering the bodies of the Syro-Phoenician women*, Adelaide: ATF Biblical Studies; Sharon Betsworth, 2010, *The Reign of God is Such as These: A socio-literary analysis of daughters in the Gospel of Mark*, London: T&T Clark.

36 Levine with Blickenstaff, 2001, p. 99.

37 Luke 1.39.

38 Luke 1.46–55.

39 Schüssler Fiorenza, 1994, p. xxviii.

40 Exodus 15.21.

41 1 Samuel 2.1–10.

42 Isaiah 61.1–2, 10.

43 Isaiah 61.11.

44 Matthew 12.46.

45 Luke 11.27.

46 Elizabeth A. Johnson, 2006, *Truly our Sister: A theology of Mary in the communion of saints*, New York: Continuum.

47 Colm Toibin, 2012, *The Testament of Mary*, London: Viking.

48 K. Barth, ET 1949, *Dogmatics in Outline*, London: SCM Press, p. 66.

13

Teaching as sacrament of salvation

Introduction

In the Introduction we considered how the Gospels seem fractured, offering us on the one hand an ethical, prophetic teacher and on the other a pre-ordained sacrificial lamb. While the teacher is seen as making mistakes, learning and growing over time, the lamb is described as spotless and eternally pre-existent. If the Christian tradition is to communicate itself successfully, it could benefit from repairing the fracture.

The word was made flesh. The fracture separates word from flesh; we need some way of reconciling them. In this chapter, we take the idea of sacraments as a place of exchange, by which we can overcome the bifurcations described above. Instead of equating Jesus' teaching solely with ethics, and his death solely with redemptive sacrifice, we can explore a theology of exchange, by which his teaching is also salvific and his death is also pedagogic. Contemporary sacramental thinking can help us in this exploration.

Sacramental theology and education

Two parallel developments have prepared the way for a perspective on teaching as a sacramental act. On the one hand, a revival of sacramental theology across several denominations has rehabilitated an aspect of Christian life and enriched it. On the other, a corresponding revival of the sacramental in Christian worship in a broad sweep of denominations has furnished the church with weekly ways of connecting ritual to belief and learning. At the same time, new theological discourses on the relationship between word and flesh, arguing the need to rebalance them so that they interrelate equally, creatively and richly, have refreshed our understanding the central Christian story.[1] They have challenged our way of thinking about the relationship between word and sacrament in Eucharist, as well as envisioning new relationships between doctrine and experience.

The experience of the church is that Jesus comes sacramentally through words and action. Taken together, words and action are a language that not only *speaks about* revelation but also *speaks* revelation.[2] The divine revelation is through words as well as actions, through ideas as well as people.[3] As the Vatican Council's statement on divine revelation, *Dei Verbum*, puts it, Christ on earth, the enfleshment of the divine, 'revealed his father and himself by deeds and words' and was 'the Incarnate Word'.[4] The same statement, discussing how the church uses Scripture in the context of liturgy, equates veneration of Scripture with veneration of the body of the Lord, both being offered equally 'from the one table of the Word of God and the Body of Christ'.[5] In branches of protestant theology, Christ is prophet, priest and king, and his embodied presence in the church is celebrated through the three roles or offices being integrated, relational and sacramental.[6]

In this renaissance of sacramental theology, we see the church reaching towards an exalted vision of sacramentality. Sacraments are 'not only the cultic expression of our thankfulness to God for salvation ... they are also, and even primarily, present mediations of this salvation',[7] in which gratitude ascends and grace descends. There are different ecclesial understandings of sacraments – what they are, how many there are, whether and how they were instituted. Sacramental theology focuses on the *idea* of sacrament, rather than the individual rites that may or may not be referred to as sacraments in the different churches. Sacraments can be seen as the ongoing mediation of the humanity of God. Using theologies of liturgy, and also theological anthropology of symbolism, Bordeyne and Morrill create a theoretical base for sacramental actions as mediating events.[8] Chauvet seeks to reinstate a sacramental way of interpreting Christian experience, charting a decline in sacramental understanding from the relatively potent idea of the symbolic through to a reduced functional or technical role, and providing resources for the revival of a wider sense of the sacramental.[9]

Here I am less concerned with *individual sacraments* as officially recognized and scripted rites, and more interested in *the sacramental* as a thread running through worship, pedagogy, and Christian communal life. Something may be sacramental – a moment, a custom, a memory – without being an official sacrament. Therefore in speaking of mediation of salvation, the Christian pedagogical imagination can conceive of hundreds of such moments, sometimes called *sacramentals*, which can be effective in this mediation. The educationalist Gert Biesta[10] sees teaching as a salvific, sacramental act, creating and recreating. There is a need to explore how this works in harmony with a theology of Christ as learning teacher.

Word made flesh – educational embodiment

In education or in mission, Christ's identity is impossible to demonstrate in the abstract, and can only be apprehended in praxis and dialogue. Doctrine alone cannot establish the titles of Christ beyond doubt or debate. The claims of Christ are best presented primarily through orthopraxy. Indeed, abstract claims of Christ's superiority or normativity as saviour can be destructive of Christianity and humanity, whereas a commitment to his teaching can and should give permission to enter into dialogue with others about the claimed titles of Christ.[11]

Since 'all the human acts of Jesus possess divine saving power', then Jesus himself, 'as the personal visible realization of the divine grace of redemption, is ... the primordial sacrament'.[12] As sign and sacrament, he is embodied, alive, relational, word made flesh. Chauvet, drawing on the natural theology of Thomas Aquinas, speaks of the symbolic efficacy of rites and points out the obvious yet overlooked insight that human bodies are sacraments and human embodiment is an 'arch-symbol' of divine presence.[13]

In the same ways that teachers and schools spend much time and energy on the physicalities of learning – pupils' attendance, their preparedness for lessons, which way they are facing in class – so Christ the sacrament's physical presence matters enormously to an understanding of his power to bring salvation. As I write, a global pandemic has triggered lockdowns, and churches are closed. Many clergy are livestreaming services. They, and the people taking part at home, even while we value the innovation, are conscious of the missing ingredient: a bodily presence to each other, and Christ's body present to us. In its absence, perhaps we appreciate its importance even more.

In this context we can consider the physicality of the incarnate word. Jesus' programme of going all about the towns and villages, healing, teaching and preaching, is the beginning of learning. In seeing the people, God senses and learns the human condition, and responds to it. Under the impact of the sights, sounds and smells of Galilee, the press and touch of its people, he is becoming a learning God.

What happens to Christ's physical body matters to our understanding of his embodied sacramental presence. His body is the subject of a sacramental exchange. It is the embodied manifestation of the divine love for humanity, and of Jesus' human love for God.[14] The start and end of his physical presence, the incarnation and ascension, complete a cycle of glorification[15] that might in our terms be called a sacramental cycle of divine and human learning.

Joseph Ratzinger detects a threefold pattern in sacraments that is also seen in the rituals in Jewish festivals: a reference to creation, a remembrance of God's action in history, and a straining forward to meet God in the future.[16] Traces of this pattern are detectable in Christian teaching too. Sacraments and sacramentals are eschatological signifiers, effective in speaking of, pointing to, and ushering in the already and the not yet of the coming kingdom. They are 'the amazed witnesses of a God who is never finished with coming'.[17]

Teaching and learning make space for this creative, salvific sacramental presence to be embodied. Christian educators can see themselves as helping students to find and live in sacramental moments as signs of the transcendent in their studies.[18] This way of seeing teaching and learning is more than a wish to inculcate Christianity: it is also about cultivating the Christian imagination so that virtually all life and learning are seen as sacramental. For example, sacramental patterns of offering, receiving, sanctifying and acting are embedded in their pedagogical steps of Thomas Groome's shared pedagogical praxis. Setting whole-person knowledge, which he calls conation,[19] as the aim of all Christian teaching, Groome identifies the naming and expressing of present practice, and critical reflection on it, as crucial first steps in praxis.[20] These correspond to the act of offering in liturgy. Groome's further steps in praxis, making the Christian story accessible and creating dialectical hermeneutics on the story, [21] could correspond to the coming of Christ through word (story) and communion (self-giving).

In this way of seeing sacramental moments, the exchange of word and flesh is potentially helpful to educators. Looking at the life of Jesus, we can recognize that teaching is a form of passionate sacrifice, and the passion on the cross is a form of teaching.

Knowledge is taken and broken

What teachers bring to the pedagogical table is the knowledge and understanding that stands behind them, which they must break open to feed the learners. What learners bring to the educational feast is the bread of their own thinking and feeling, bread to be broken. In either case, there is something to be broken open and shared. Teachers often speak of breaking down content; the teacher's planning mind allots portions of content, making rapid, complex judgements about the best size, richness and sequence. For adult learners as well as children, it is often necessary to unlearn before new learning can take place. The Christian educator Jeff Astley observes this necessity while also regretting the damage it can sometimes do:

> Christian learning is partly ophthalmic. It involves a correction of vision, a change in people's way of seeing ... Or at least it could. Much Christian and academic theological teaching, however, seeks wholly to raze people's pre-existing theological fabrications to the ground, trampling their personal narratives and imaginative images, before attempting (often unsuccessfully) to build something entirely new and unrelated on the bulldozed site.[22]

This rather distressing metaphor does not deny that breaking is needed, and breaking is destructive. The word 'fabrications' in Astley's metaphor – suggesting temporary intellectual structures, theological habitations for a family of faith – invites the idea that all such theology is temporary, and is open to adaptation, if not destruction. One thinks of the school chaplain addressing the Year 7s in Chapter 2. There are degrees of destructiveness and there is Christian and professional judgement about the degree warranted. The breaking open of word and flesh involves breaking open our own fabrications too.

Most theology, whether ordinary or academic, is already broken. The fragmentary and unsystematic nature of thinking about Jesus' identity and work, and the ways in which people reconcile it with their daily lives – changeably, awkwardly at times – has been described as a 'bits-and-pieces' theology.[23] Jesus' teaching in the synoptics could be said to have a similarly fragmented character, the result of an oral tradition being sifted and mixed by communities. However provisional and untidy these theologies may seem, however broken, they can and do nourish discipleship in the form of Christian action in the world. There is a 'depth grammar'[24] of broken theology made manifest in how lives are lived.

An adult Christian learner reflects on breaking and remaking thus: 'As I get older, I'm more willing to question ... but oddly, my faith seems deeper too.'[25] Christians who are willing to take the risk of breaking open their assumptions and moving have a sacramental sensibility unafraid of breaking. A different form of tearing and breaking is envisaged by the powerful image of adult theological educators as 'midwife teachers' who enable learners to give birth to new ideas.[26]

Kierkegaard described teaching and learning as a 'breaking asunder', in a poetic passage that owes much to Jesus' parables and hints at the divine inevitability of the breaking:

> When the seed of the oak is planted in earthen vessels, they break asunder; when new wine is poured in old leather bottles, they burst; what must happen when the God implants himself in human weakness, unless man becomes a new vessel and a new creature! But this becoming, what labors will attend the change, how convulsed with birth-pangs! And the understanding – how precarious, and how close each moment to misunderstanding, when the anguish of guilt seeks to disturb the peace of love! And how rapt in fear; for it is indeed less terrible to fall to the ground when the mountains tremble at the voice of the God, than to sit at table with him as an equal; and yet it is the God's concern precisely to have it so.[27]

In the same way that many sacraments begin their ritual with a reference to the materials of creation – the waters of baptism, the bread and wine of Eucharist, the oil of anointing, the human love of matrimony – so a sacramental understanding of teaching sees it as an act of creation. Learning, whether by assimilation or accommodation, is a tiny act of shaping the world anew, bringing order out of chaos. It is 'a progressive process ... through which the individual, the community of faith and, conceivably, the culture is gradually formed in its image of humanity and understanding of God'.[28] The doctrine of creation itself is 'the opening of a word',[29] the initiation of a continuing logos. It is a continuing creative act. Even in the midst of breaking – because learning does often enough mean the loss of former models – creativity is present.

But we should also turn this thought on its head. Teaching, whether by Jesus or anyone else, does not always bring order out of chaos: often enough it does the reverse, disrupting the ordered world of the learner, shaking their mental models, by introducing new knowledge or a new layer of complexity. We see this in Jesus' repeated 'You have heard it said ... but I tell you ...'[30] statements, discussed in Chapter 7. A sacramental way of understanding teaching is that it sets up a virtually ceaseless dialectic between creating and breaking, breaking and recreating.

So we can see in the history and practice of Christian education a regular usage of the imagery of breaking and recreating. Jesus as a teacher breaks open the Scripture: the Torah in his hands is opened, examined, its conventional received meanings destroyed, new meanings created and offered. He breaks open the signs of the times – the lived experience of communities. In doing so, he creates a kingdom. Then he does the same with his own body. His teaching is sacramental.

Teaching as sacrifice, sacrifice as teaching

Teachers enjoy the 'win' of seeing a learner break into new realizations. Teaching and being understood is glorious – it is victory, love, success. They also suffer the 'defeat' of failure when a learner does not engage or achieve. Such victories and defeats are common in every day of a teacher's life. Jesus experienced this, and more: the risk of placing his teaching into hands that would distort it, the crucifixion of being deliberately misunderstood or misinterpreted. In his case, teaching and being misunderstood – misquoted, trapped, falsely accused – brought a fresh sense of sacrifice. The crucial Gospel text that can shed light on this is Jesus' critical incident question, analysed in Chapter 10 ('How shall we picture the kingdom?'[31]). It is here that we glimpse the mind of a teacher who realizes that his work is being malignly and cruelly broken, just as his body would be broken on the cross.

Just as his teaching is a form of sacrifice, so his ultimate sacrifice of his life is a form of teaching. I do not mean to restate the soteriological theory that his death atones by being a moral example of self-sacrifice – a theory offered by Kant and critiqued by Pannenberg as of 'modest'[32] soteriological interest. Instead, I am looking for a deeper reciprocity between teaching and atonement, one that unites the two, seeing the cross as a kind of logos, a piece of teaching.[33]

From the cross, just as he so often did before, Jesus teaches from Scripture: His cry to God about abandonment[34] is usually interpreted as an expression of hellish suffering, and it certainly is that, but probably more: a use of Scripture to pose a question to humanity and God about the dark heart of our suffering. Swallowed up and destroyed by pain, he is still a learning teacher, whose question is on behalf of all humanity and God. 'The cross promises that the resentment and rage of the sufferer need not be denied or repressed, since ... Jesus too shouted his frustration in the face of God.'[35] Jesus has learnt how far human cruelty can go, and his teaching comes from his learning.

His cry of abandonment is a piece of teaching in another sense, which is also characteristic of his earlier teaching. It is a statement about the righteousness, power and holiness of God. If he had had breath, would he have continued reciting Psalm 22 to its end?

> The whole earth, from end to end, will remember and come back to Yahweh; all the families of the nations will bow down before him. For Yahweh reigns, the ruler of nations![36]

In that moment on the cross, this affirmation of God's holiness, righteousness and power would have been in Jesus' memory even though not on his tongue. Thus the cross teaches God's presence even when God seems absent, God's power even when God seems powerless. 'What the silence of God on Good Friday discloses, in light of Easter dawn, is not the indifference of God but the difference of God, God's otherness ... God's holiness.'[37]

The cry of abandonment is, therefore, a uniquely condensed and dramatic piece of teaching, characteristic of Jesus' pedagogy: posing a question and proposing a profound faith in God. Whether or not Jesus predicted and intended his death, the cross is a teaching event in continuity with his teachings. The mysterious core of the gospel is that both the teaching and the passion are forms of breaking, beautifully courageous and hideously wasteful; yet both lead to forms of recreating through an alliance of word and flesh. Thus the teaching life and teaching death of Jesus are a saving sacrifice, not the death solely.[38]

Sacred, saving, embodied, a teaching presence in life and death: Jesus' actions are sacraments, lifting every aspect of human life into sacramentality, 'for the sanctification of humanity and the well-being of the world'.[39] The educator and theologian Mary Elizabeth Mullino Moore shares her vision and practice of the full scope of sacramentality in teaching, seeing it as a quality that works for 'reconstruction and repair'[40] after the breaking. One of the most important acts of sacramental teaching is to 'remember the dismembered',[41] those broken apart by division, oppression, or abuse. This involves facing pain: Moore describes a 'wrenching event'[42] that took place in one of her own theology classes, and the quick professional and personal decisions she had to make as the teacher. The event involved one student's painful remembrance of witnessing a violent attack on her mother. From this and similar professional experiences, Moore is able to build a 'hermeneutic of tragic memory'[43] by which learners follow a sacramental pattern: first engaging in the remembrance of a painful past, next confronting in themselves the dynamics of suffering, and then through reflection reaching some form of resolution that enables an individual and a community to step forward. Filaments of this pattern – story, reflection, pain and sacrifice, resolution – are embedded in tiny ways in the repeated steps of everyday teaching: recall, routine, the pain and fear of a new challenge, and progress achieved.

In interpreting teaching as characterized in part by a hermeneutic of pain, Moore is markedly countercultural and courageous, showing in her account of her experiences that a teacher's responses to painful challenges are always instinctive, split-second, and rarely wholly right or wholly wrong. Where John Hull warns of the major blockage to adult Christian education being 'the need to be right and the pain of learning',[44] Moore constructs a sacramental narrative of learning to embrace the pain, thereby deepening the learning. What she achieves is a repairing of the original fracture between the word of new learning and the flesh of experience.

Conclusion

If we place the patterns of sacramentality alongside the routines of teaching, some interesting and fruitful parallels emerge. They both call into being a new creation; they break and repair; they face the pain and risk of new interpretations, new insights, nudging aside the old; they signify and achieve an encounter between word and flesh; they see redeeming hope in Jesus' salvific teaching as much as in his pedagogic death; and thus they begin to reunify the fractured text of the Gospels. In the Christian pedagogical imagination, to notice these resemblances day by day, to live them without necessarily seeking or forcing them, constitutes the beginnings of a sacramental form of teaching. In the remembering and imagining, he is there, burning in our hearts.

Notes

1 Claire Henderson Davis, 2007, *After the Church: Divine encounter in a sexual age*, Norwich: Canterbury Press.

2 Gerald O'Collins, 2016, *Revelation: Towards a Christian interpretation of God's self-revelation in Jesus Christ*, Oxford: Oxford University Press, p. 44.

3 O'Collins, 2016, p. 54.

4 Austin Flannery (ed.), 1975, '*Dei Verbum*, Dogmatic Constitution on Divine Revelation', in *Vatican Council II*, Dublin: Dominican Publications, pp. 750–65, p. 760.

5 Flannery, 1975, p. 762.

6 Richard Belcher, 2016, *Prophet, Priest and King: The roles of Christ in the bible and our roles today*, Phillipsburg, NJ: P and R Publishing; J. Scott Duvall and J. Daniel Hays, 2019, *God's Relational*

Presence: The cohesive centre of biblical theology, Grand Rapids, MI: Baker Academic.

7 Louis Marie Chauvet, 1994, *Symbol and Sacrament: Sacramental reinterpretation of Christian experience*, New York: Pueblo Publishing Company, p. 10.

8 Philippe Bordeyne and Bruce T. Morrill (eds), 2009, *Sacraments: Revelation of the humanity of God*, Collegeville, MN: Liturgical Press.

9 Chauvet, 1994.

10 Gert Biesta, 2016, *The Beautiful Risk of Education*, London and New York: Routledge.

11 A. Hennelly, 1995, *Liberation Theologies: The global pursuit of justice*, Mystic, CT: Twenty-third Publications, p. 306.

12 Edward Schillebeeckx, 2014, *Collected Works, Volume 1: Christ the sacrament of the encounter with God*, London: T&T Clark, p. 11.

13 Chauvet, 1994, p. 151.

14 Schillebeeckx, 2014, p. 42.

15 Schillebeeckx, 2014, p. 17.

16 J. Ratzinger, 2007, *Jesus of Nazareth*, London: Bloomsbury, p. 307.

17 Chauvet, 1994, p. 555.

18 Karen Eifler and Thomas Landy, 2014, *Becoming beholders: Cultivating sacramental imagination and actions in college classrooms*, Collegeville, MN: The Liturgical Press.

19 Thomas Groome, 1991, *Sharing faith: A comprehensive approach to religious education and pastoral ministry: The way of shared praxis*, San Francisco, CA: HarperCollins, p. 11.

20 Groome, 1991, pp. 175ff.

21 Groome, 1991, pp. 215ff.

22 Jeff Astley, 2013, 'Ordinary theology and the learning conversation with academic theology', in Jeff Astley and Leslie Francis (eds), *Exploring Ordinary Theology: Everyday Christian believing and the church*, Farnham: Ashgate, pp. 44–54, pp. 51–2.

23 Ann Christie, 2013, 'Jesus as exemplar', in Astley and Francis (eds), pp. 77–85, p. 80.

24 Christie, 2013, p. 84.

25 Helen Savage, 2013, 'Ordinary learning', in Astley and Francis (eds), pp. 199–208, p. 202.

26 Savage, 2013, p. 205.

27 Howard V. Hong and Edna H. Hong (eds), 1985, *Søren Kierkegaard: Philosophical fragments*, Princeton, NJ: Princeton University Press, p. 27.

28 David Heywood, 2004, *Divine Revelation and Human Learning: A Christian theory of knowledge*, Aldershot: Ashgate, p. 166.

29 Chauvet, 1994, p. 551.

30 Matthew 5.38ff.

31 Mark 4.30.

32 Wolfhart Pannenberg, ET 1968, *Jesus – God and Man*, London: SCM Press, p. 45.

33 Chauvet, 1994, p. 4.

34 Mark 15.34; Psalm 22.2.

35 Leander E. Keck, 2000, *Who is Jesus? History in perfect tense*, Columbia, SC: University of South Carolina Press, p. 149.

36 Psalm 22.27–28.

37 Keck, 2000, p. 134.

38 Chauvet, 1994, p. 297.

39 Mary Elizabeth Mullino Moore, 2004, *Teaching as a Sacramental Act*, Cleveland, OH: Pilgrim Press.

40 Moore, 2004, p. 206.

41 Moore, 2004, p. 38.

42 Moore, 2004, p. 65.

43 Moore, 2004, p. 77.

44 John Hull, 1985, *What Prevents Christian Adults from Learning?*, London: SCM Press, pp. 89ff.

14

Towards an educational economy of the Trinity and the church

Introduction

If Jesus is a learning teacher, and if his humanity is that of a lifelong learner, what are the implications of this for Christian belief in his divinity, and for his presence in the church? Does the son bring learning into the Trinity? And the vulnerability and mistake-making that goes with learning? How far do learning and change extend into the heart of the life of the Triune God and into the church? How does the theology of incarnation influence Christian educational work?

Here I propose that the learning Christ draws his own into the life of the Trinity, which becomes in itself a learning community. The Triune God has an economy – a way of being itself to the world – that includes teaching and learning. The church, imitating and reflecting the divine three-in-one, should have a learning economy.

A divine economy

Christian theologians use the term 'economy' in relation to the Trinity in a specific way. It derives from *oikonomia*, denoting management or stewardship of a household. Paul applies the concept to the unfolding of a divine plan for the whole world.[1] Some theologians make a distinction between the *economic* Trinity – the way the Triune God appears to humanity and creation – and the *immanent* Trinity, the way the Triune God is in God's self, ontologically. For example, the economic Trinity is present in the life of the church, through the sacraments, fellowship and worship, as well as through mutual giving and receiving in relationships. Creation and salvation history are also powerful loci for the presence and action of the Trinity. All these more or less tangible manifestations can be said to be evidence of the three-in-one with us, almost literally a cashing out, into the whole world and the household of faith, of what it means to be a Triune God. Moltmann holds this economic Trinity to be God's way of being open to the world in time and place.[2]

Now a Triune God cannot have one set of defining characteristics economically and a different set ontologically or immanently, even if the difference is slight. Mackey warned of the danger in such a distinction, particularly if it leaves little room for a meaningful language to describe persons in the Godhead.[3] Rahner adhered to a formula that the economic Trinity is the immanent Trinity, 'and *vice versa*'.[4] The way God appears, and what God does, is who God is. Boff had it that 'the way God comes to meet human beings is the way in which God subsists'.[5]

The educational salience of the economic idea lies in its challenge to dominant notions of the Triune God as static and unlearning. The idea of an eternal, unchanging father who sends his son to earth, and a son who returns to take his seat at the father's right hand, cannot live easily with the dynamism of an economic Trinity that is identical with the true nature of God. That the returning son carries his wounds, we know; but too often he appears in other ways unchanged by his incarnation, and unable to change his father. He is too much like a son returning from his gap year abroad amid poverty and oppression, having had an 'amazing' time, but now resuming his former life and not seeking to challenge his family's assumptions. That is an insipid model of the Trinity, too much influenced by patriarchal models of capitalist power: monarchic, an 'a-Trinitarian monotheism', individualistic and powerless to make change.[6] It is also a Trinity having none of the internal dynamism of which Augustine taught, when he distinguished between the three persons and enumerated how they complement each other:

> There is the Father and the Son and the Holy Spirit – each of these is God, and all of them together are one God … The Father is neither the Son nor the Holy Spirit, the Son is neither the Father nor the Holy Spirit, the Holy Spirit is neither the Father nor the Son, but the Father is purely the Father, the Son purely the Son, and the Holy Spirit purely the Holy Spirit … And the three are all one because of the Father, all equal because of the Son, and all in harmony because of the Holy Spirit.[7]

Augustine worked his way carefully through the problem of the Trinity's unchanging nature and the change made by the begotten, incarnate son. His task was to systematize the untidy scriptural evidence for the Trinity, and to confute heretical versions of it. Of each of the three persons, Augustine taught that they are fully God, and share all the characteristics of God, yet are not each other. The three together are unchanging, 'one being and one greatness and one truth and one wisdom … but not … together one Word',[8] because among them, between them, there is movement and dynamism. In the three-in-one, then, there is room for the 'mutual acceptance of differences' that can form the 'vehicle for the plural unity of the three divine Persons'.[9] Relationality exists as a characteristic of the Trinity; because of the ways in which the three Persons relate to each other, personhood and relationality are complementary;[10] and since the church, modelled on the Trinity, is 'the eschatological gathering of the entire people of God in the communion of the triune God',[11] that complementarity must be a hallmark of church life too.

One of the central theological principles from Augustine's period was coined by his contemporary Gregory of Nazianzus: the unassumed is the unhealed.[12] That is, what God assumes or embraces on earth becomes healed and raised up in the new dispensation. The incarnation must immerse God completely in human existence in order to raise humanity to be part of the triune divinity. Speaking of suffering, the theologian Paul Fiddes defines the lesson thus: 'If God's suffering is to be of healing effect for a suffering world, then it must be recognizably God's, and not merely our human suffering projected on to God.'[13] Moltmann adds: 'My interpretation of the death of Christ ... is not as an event between God and man, but primarily as an event within the Trinity.'[14] The suffering of abandonment happens within the Trinity.

Surely the same is true of God's learning. God's absolute freedom, defended passionately in the Lutheran and Calvinist traditions, includes the freedom to suffer, to love and to learn. And Fiddes adds that God has no self other than suffering – no inner temple in which God's essence is protected from suffering. God's otherness from us is an 'otherness in suffering'.[15] Again, as with suffering so with learning: God's learning is of the very essence, not merely a manifest element; God's learning is as eternal as the Trinity, bound up with the inner and outer relationality of the Trinity. God's learning is not at the expense of divine knowledge, power or immutability. God learns, and yet remains God.

To this complex system of trinitarian balances and distinctions, an educator brings the realization that Christ the incarnate Word, a learning teacher, is the same economically as he is ontologically. Therefore Christ is a learning teacher in the life of the Trinity, and since the Trinity is one, Christ brings learning and teaching into the very heart of God. We might paraphrase Augustine's words thus:

All of them together are one God; each of them is a full substance and all together are one substance. The Father does not know everything the Son or the Holy Spirit know; the Son does not learn everything the Father and the Holy Spirit learn; the Holy Spirit does not teach everything the Father and the Son teach. All three are one because they know, learn and teach as one.

To an educator's eye, what springs from this inner structure and outward manifestation of the Trinity is its collegiality, its dynamic and eternal conversation. But to be salient in teaching and learning terms, the Trinity's inner dynamism should be more visible to the church in preaching and practice.

What a learning Trinity shows to a learning church

For building a bridge between the economic Trinity as a learning community and the church, there are already many raw materials. First we should deal with the question of gendered language, since this has the capacity to invalidate the concept of the Trinity from having any educational significance. The predominantly masculine language traditionally used by theology to describe the Trinity strikes oddly on modern ears. The issue here is not a theological one about women and men, or the nature of God – issues dealt with extensively by other writers[16] – but a more technical question about how an economic Trinity, impacting on teaching and learning, can and should be verbalized in the service of a learning church. Gendered language should be questioned as part of this discussion, since an all-male Trinity, or nearly all-male, tends to disable theological language from grasping the all-encompassing nature of God's being (assuming that any language ever can). More importantly, such language tends to imply that men are closer to God than women, and has been used for this purpose; thus implicitly or explicitly excluding some worshippers.

There have been feminist translations – 'Mother, lover, friend' who is transcendent, immanent, and mediator, from Sallie McFague;[17] 'Life-giver, pain-bearer, love-maker' from Jim Cotter;[18] and a counter-translation from Janet Martin Soskice, who argues that the triune language is already effectively feminist because the triadic structure rejects binaries, rises above the notion of 'the other' as 'not me', and is inherently relational.[19] Soskice sees in trinitarian language the recovery of an original intention to speak of an embodied God, and holds this to be of more importance than the gender of the language used. Hannah Bacon[20] shifts the focus from language to thinking and experience, picturing ways in which the three-in-one reflects women's experience. There is also Augustine's formulation of lover, beloved and love,[21] which he suggests may have the same triadic structure in our minds as the Trinity does. What we can note here is that alternative, inclusive language and conceptualizing for the three-in-one exists, that it retains and perhaps strengthens the inner dynamism and relationality of the Triune God, and has refreshed Christian thinking and spirituality in relation to the three members of the Trinity. This is an important part of the raw materials for reconnecting the doctrine to educational purposes.

Next we should attempt to discern what characteristics of the economic Trinity can be placed in the service of a learning economy in the church. Three such characteristics spring from orthodox and modern formulations of trinitarian language: that the Trinity is clearly dynamic, discursive and desiring. The dynamism of the Trinity's immanent life is well attested in ancient and contemporary writing, and finds its supporting counterparts in synoptic accounts of Jesus as actor, disruptor and change-maker, and in Paul's description of the mind of Christ. The discursive nature of God's three-in-one-ness finds its expression in a continuing open invitation to all creation to participate in a conversation, for example in parables that deal with God's dialogue with people such as the tenants in the vineyard and the servants at the wedding feast. Mutual desire, understood as loving interest given and received, is found in the trinitarian language of love, and has strong resonance with the Johannine literature's frequent mentions of Jesus' closeness with his disciples.

Dynamism in Trinity and church

The dynamism of the Trinity is directed at us and at all beings in creation. It is described in Paul's portrayal of the mind of Christ, in his letter to the Philippians: his 'state was divine, yet he did not cling to his equality with God'.[22] This passage, sometimes referred to as kenotic theology (*kenosis*, self-emptying), is probably an early church hymn, a word picture of the descent of Christ to humanity, to humility, to death, death on a cross – and of his re-ascent, raised on high, given a name above all other names ('Lord'), so that all beings should bend the knee to him, and every tongue acclaim him 'to the glory of God the Father'.[23] The beautiful downwards-upwards trajectory painted by this passage starts and ends with Jesus' membership of the Trinity. The life of the threefold Godhead is not forgotten in the middle of the passage: the Trinity is drawn downwards, as it were, to embrace suffering and humiliation. And if suffering and humiliation, then why not learning too, since it is so evidently a dimension of human existence and a part of Jesus' earthly life? Paul might just as relevantly have written:

> In your intellectual life you must be the same as Christ Jesus: his position was authoritative, yet he did not insist on an all-knowing status, but emptied himself, to assume the condition of a learner, and became as all human learners are, in time and place; and being as all human learners are, he was humbler yet, even to accepting the crucifixion of misunderstanding, a misunderstanding caused by wilful blindness. Yet God raised him high ...

It is through a textual adaptation of this sort, perhaps, that we see the fully radical and subversive nature of the Trinity's dynamism directed towards our life and our theological structures, many of which are upended by the direction of this energy.

Paul's letter counsels humility, in imitation of Christ. He exhorts them to think like Christ.[24] In this context the verb 'to think', or 'to have in mind' (*phroneite*, from *phroneo*), can also mean 'to think the thoughts of' or 'to be in harmony of mind with' Christ. Expressing it in such a way makes the passage potentially more than a moral exhortation to think humbly towards each other because Christ was humble: it could also mean *to have the mind of Christ* in his kenotic fall and rise, *to be in vital union with Christ's attitude* of learning and humility, and thus to be drawn into the learning life of the Trinity.

In few other places in Scripture do we see the dynamism of trinitarian theology so powerfully expressed, its economic and educational implications for the church so brushed over by subsequent use. Potentially, the Trinity's dynamism offers us a radical insight. David Heywood, in his study of revelation and learning, argues from the nature of learning. If, following pedagogical science, learning means the learner's mind acting on some information, and if the information is thereby changed by assimilation into the mental models of the learner; then learning changes both the learner and that which is learned. Applied to the Trinity as a mutual learning community, it suggests that the Triune God is changed by learning and by being learnt; the kenoticism draws the Trinity into change – an insight that, as Heywood puts it, has 'potentially an enormous impact on theology'.[25]

The economy of the church has not always lived up to trinitarian dynamism. For one expert in developing parish life, hallmarks of a healthy church life should include openness to change and a credit in 'the memory bank of change',[26] in other words, having the kenotic mind of Christ when it comes to learning new things. By contrast, a church that lacks or underpowers the learning dynamism of Christ could be called an unlearning church, and John Hull warns of its capacity to inflict a deathly boredom:

It is strange how slowly and irresistibly the realization that one is infinitely bored creeps up and assassinates the contemporary church-goer ... The realization sets up a further kind of cognitive dissonance. The worship of God ought to be a joy. But it is a bore ... Boredom is to the religious consciousness what pain is to the physical body. It is the warning that something is wrong. It is one of the ways in which the crushed energies of the spirit defend themselves against the creeping moribundity of the unlearning personality.[27]

Discursiveness in Trinity and church

The economy of the Trinity may be said to be discursive because its distinct Persons are in relationship and conversation with each other – a conversation into which all beings are invited. The significant difference between monologue and conversation is a power issue. Just as Christ did not cling to equal status with God, so triune conversation is equal. Cunningham's notion of 'trinitarian practice'[28] – a language and doctrine shaped by the practices of a believing community – includes the practice of persuading: 'God and human beings are engaged in a process of mutual persuasion'.[29] Persuasion is the opposite of compulsion. It reminds us, too, of how Jesus as a teacher could at times impress his hearers, not through rank but through the intrinsic authority of his words.

By contrast, oppressive uses of power can be caused or exacerbated by unequal distribution of knowledge. Where an economy produces among its people conditions of 'opiatic resignation', 'capitulation before injustice' or 'pure abdication',[30] this can be because educational transactions have been one-way, rather than dialectical. For theologians working in contexts of oppression, faith is real if it is dialectical – it is worked out by continuing conversation until it produces the justice of the kingdom and ends deception.[31] Dialectical faith fits the church to be an image of the discursive Trinity.

We have seen many examples, discussed in Part 2, of the dialectics employed by Jesus. One educator, Thomas Groome, writes that the church can employ a 'pedagogy of God', a 'pedagogy of Jesus' and a 'pedagogy of the incarnation',[32] by which he means a participatory experience in which each person is an active subject, reading their own and each other's experience in the life of the church, in a continuing dialectic (like the three Persons). The title of his work – 'Handing on the faith: The need for total catechetical education' – is a hint that he believes this discursive characteristic needs to be a hallmark of the totality of the church. Other educators share the belief and add that the vitality, mission and even the survival of the church depend on establishing effective adult education.[33] In

Jane Regan's description of a new paradigm for adult theological education at parish level, it is interesting to note her
reference to the language of economy – how much money was
spent on education, how decisions were made on educational
effort, who was employed in doing what, and what had to
change in the process of creating and recreating a learning
community.[34] We see here that the dynamism and discursiveness of a church, when it reflects the learning economy of the
three-in-one, has material manifestations. Regan adds that in
her experience few adults have the opportunity to engage with
this vitality, and she is joined by other researcher-practitioners
who have raised their concern that the discursive economy
tends to be neglected.[35]

Desire in Trinity and church

The trinitarian characteristic of mutual desire is a hallmark of
a learning economy in the church. We are taught that it is love
that holds Augustine's conception of the Trinity together and
draws all creation into the life of the divine. God's desire for us,
and our desiring response, form an implicit aspect of the sacraments of initiation that transform the lives of individuals and
invite them more deeply into the life of Christ.[36] Therefore, a
church with a strong educational economy is one that educates
heart as well as mind, a pattern that can be seen in successful
historical examples from Christianity and Judaism.[37]

James Smith, writing on Christian educational practices,
imagines the church's liturgy as a conversation between lover
and beloved, a representation and ritual of mutual desire
between Christ and those who belong to him. The ritual, to
deepen love, requires repetition and practice.[38] The practice of
this desire is also dialectical – a repeated pattern of formation,
misformation and counter-formation, between practices that
can turn our hearts away from Christ and those that can orient
us towards him.[39] The rituals and practices need to be 'thick',
that is, rich in their depth and complexity, and in their capacity

to form our identity, 'get hold of our core desire – our ultimate love that defines us'.[40]

Desire means a teacher's hunger to enable learners to grow in understanding, and a learner's deep longing to take what the teacher offers. In Jesus' dealings with his disciples, and particularly with John and Mary Magdalene, we have seen this mutual desire at its most intense. The depth and intimacy of these desiring exchanges in the Gospels has embarrassed the church. Church authorities and some theologians have allowed themselves to be distracted by the question of whether the desire in those cases was sexual, was consummated, was same-sex or opposite-sex, and so on; authorities have taken fright and denied it, radical theologians have become excited and asserted it. That quarrel has thrown our vision out of balance. The vibrancy of the Trinity's desire for us, in harmony with the dynamism and discursiveness that make for intimate conversation and honest learning, is neither sexual nor chaste, or perhaps it is both; it is passionate, it is powerful, it is indecent, in Marcella Althaus-Reid's sense,[41] because it shocks those who adhere to a static, unlearning Trinity.

Does today's church, reflecting the divine economy, deeply desire learning for all its members? Several practitioners of education have equivocal or critical responses.[42] Being exposed to the questions of the young, the marginalized, the laity, is a salutary discipline for any theological system, reflecting Jesus' own focus on the young as inheritors of the kingdom.

How a flourishing educational economy works

Each tradition is diverse in the strength of its educational economy: 'each has its scholars, each its book-burners; each has its eras of prodigious scholarly energy and intellectual daring, each its periods of introversion and dry dogmatism'.[43] The measures of a strong educational economy are closely related to how Jesus taught, as well as the immanent life of the Trinity. The measures could include a flexible, subtle, rigorous and vital hermeneutics, with an acknowledgement of diversity and dissonance within the tradition; a positive, hospitable disposition towards questioning and critical enquiry, with a courageous outlook on all its risks and perils; and a capacity to create a rationale for theological and ethical change. In a healthy economy, theology is goaded into creativity, realism, and a dialectic of tradition and innovation. Churches have been given a theological treasure. To preserve theological wealth, they must speculate in the educational market. Take the treasure out of the vault. Bring from the storeroom things new and old.[44]

The educational economy is an investment in mission. Faced with modernity and diversity, this investment must be more courageous than the attempt to 'salvage some old truth or other'.[45] It needs to include new understandings and models of ministry in all churches, to rebalance the patriarchal emphasis in theology. The theologian Claire Henderson Davis, in her open letter to Pope Francis,[46] urges the church to make connections between the ecological message of *Laudato Si*'[47] and the process of recovering and restoring Christianity from patriarchal influences. She calls for a new way of educating and forming priests and ministers.

Will our children have faith? John Westerhoff acknowledges the timeless salience of the question, and in conclusion points to the economy of the church – particularly its capacity to create space for conversation – as the source of a good solution:

> Will our children have faith? Only if we adults have faith and share it with our children ... If we care about the next generation we will worry about our own. The place to begin is with ourselves.[48]

Westerhoff might have added that the place to begin, in ourselves, is with our depth of understanding, and how well it is permitted, encouraged and resourced in the economy of the churches we attend.

Notes

1 Ephesians 1.10; 3.9.

2 Jürgen Moltmann, ET 1981, *The Trinity and the Kingdom*, London: SCM Press, p. 94.

3 James Mackey, 1995, 'Social Models of the Trinity', in R. Gill (ed.), *Readings in Modern Theology*, London: SPCK, pp. 123–30.

4 Kark Rahner, ET 1970, *The Trinity*, London: Burnes and Oates, p. 22.

5 Leonardo Boff, ET 1988, *Trinity and Society*, Maryknoll, NY: Orbis Books, p. 95.

6 Boff, 1988, p. 148.

7 Augustine, *On Christian Teaching*, Book 1: 11–12.

8 Augustine, *On the Trinity*, Book 7: 3.

9 Boff, 1988, p. 150.

10 J. Bracken, 1974, 'The holy trinity as a community of divine persons', *Heythrop Journal* 15, pp. 166–82.

11 Miroslav Volf, 1998, *After our Likeness: The church as the image of the Trinity*, Grand Rapids, MI: Eerdmans, p. 257.

12 Gregory of Nazianzus, 380, *An Examination of Apollinarianism*, Book 101.

13 Paul Fiddes, 1988, *The Creative Suffering of God*, Oxford: Clarendon Press, p. 110.

14 Jürgen Moltmann, 1995, 'The crucified God', in Johann-Baptist Metz and Jürgen Moltmann, *Faith and the Future: Essays on theology, solidarity, and modernity*, Maryknoll, NY: Orbis Books, pp. 89–99, p. 96.

15 Fiddes, 1988, p. 142.

16 Mary E. Hunt and Dianne L. Neu (eds), 2012, *New Feminist Christianity: Many voices, many views*, Nashville, TN: SkyLight Paths Publishing.

17 Sallie McFague, 1987, *Models of God: Theology for an ecological, nuclear age*, Minneapolis, MN: Fortress Press.

18 Jim Cotter and Paul Payton, 2006, *Out of the Silence – Into the Silence: Prayer's daily round*, Harlech: Cairns Publications, p. 505.

19 Janet Martin Soskice, 2002, 'The Trinity and feminism', in Susan Frank Parsons (ed.), *The Cambridge Companion to Feminist Theology*, Cambridge: Cambridge University Press, pp. 135–50, p. 140.

20 Hannah Bacon, 2016, *What's Right with the Trinity? Conversations in feminist theology*, Abingdon: Routledge.

21 Augustine, *On the Trinity*, Chapter 2: 2.

22 Philippians 2.5–11.

23 Philippians 2.11.

24 Philippians 2.5.

TOWARDS AN EDUCATIONAL ECONOMY

25 David Heywood, 2004, *Divine Revelation and Human Learning: A Christian theory of knowledge*, Aldershot: Ashgate, p. 31.

26 Robert Warren, 2004, *The Healthy Churches' Handbook*, London: Church House Publishing, p. 34.

27 John Hull, 1985, *What Prevents Christian Adults from Learning?*, London: SCM Press, p. 137.

28 David Cunningham, 1998, *These Three are One: The practice of trinitarian theology*, Oxford: Blackwell, pp. 1ff.

29 Cunningham, 1998, p. 306.

30 José Miranda, ET 1977, *Marx and the Bible: A critique of the philosophy of oppression*, London: SCM Press, p. 280.

31 Miranda, 1977, pp. 201–2, 233.

32 Thomas Groome, 2006, 'Handing on the faith: The need for total catechetical education', in Robert Imbelli (ed.), *Handing on the Faith: The church's mission and challenge*, New York: Crossroad Publishing Company, pp. 172–92, pp. 188–9.

33 Jane Regan, 2002, *Toward an Adult Church: A vision of faith formation*, Chicago, IL: Loyola Press; Jeff Astley (ed.), 2000, *Learning in the Way: Research and reflection on adult Christian education*, Leominster: Gracewing.

34 Regan, 2002.

35 John Elias, 1982, *The Foundations and Practice of Adult Religious Education*, Malabar, FL: Robert E. Krieger Publishing; John Paver, 2016, *Theological Reflection and Education for Ministry: The search for integration in theology*, Abingdon: Routledge; Frances Ward, 2005, *Lifelong Learning: Theological reflection and supervision*, London: SCM Press.

36 Robert Imbelli, 2006, 'Introduction: discernment, newness, transformation: musings inspired by a conference', in Imbelli (ed.), pp. 1–9.

37 John van Engen (ed.), 2004, *Educating People of Faith: Exploring the history of Jewish and Christian communities*, Grand Rapids, MI: Eerdmans.

38 James Smith, 2009, *Desiring the Kingdom: Worship, worldview, and cultural formation*, Grand Rapids, MI: Baker Academic, pp. 39ff.

39 Smith, 2009, p. 88.

40 Smith, 2009, p. 85.

41 Marcella Althaus-Reid, 2000, *Indecent Theology: Theological perversions in sex, gender and politics*, London: Routledge.

42 M. Mayr (ed.), 1988, *Does the Church Really Want Religious Education?*, Birmingham, AL: RE Press; Patrick Devitt, 1991, *How Adult is Adult Religious Education?*, Dublin: Veritas.

43 Mark Chater and Clive Erricker, 2013, *Does Religious Education have a Future? Pedagogical and policy prospects*, Abingdon: Routledge, p. 124.

44 Matthew 13.52.

45 Jürgen Habermas, 1996, 'Philosopher as stand-in and interpreter', in J. Appleby, E. Covington, D, Hoyt, M. Latham and A. Sneider (eds), *Knowledge and Postmodernism in Historical Perspective*, London and New York: Routledge, pp. 514–15.

46 Claire Henderson Davis, 2020, 'An Easter love letter to Pope Francis', *The Tablet*, 11 April, 274(9347), online at www.thetablet. co.uk/features/2/17848/an-easter-love-letter-to-pope-francis.

47 Pope Francis, 2015, *Laudato Si'*, *Encyclical Letter on Care for our Common Home*, Rome: The Vatican, 24 May, online at www.vatican.va/content/francesco/en/encyclicals/documents/papa-francesco_20150524_enciclica-laudato-si.html.

48 John H. Westerhoff III, 1976, *Will our Children have Faith?* New York: Morehouse Publishing, p. 174.

Postscript and proposals: Where pedagogy and theology meet

Introduction

What difference does it make to look at Jesus Christ as a learning teacher? In Part 1 we discovered how this kind of looking differs from conventional discourses, whether theologies of education or Christologies; in Part 2 we observed new facets of Jesus as a teacher – new, that is, in the sense that they were partially obscured in normative readings of the Gospels. Where the Gospels leave us, with a fragmentary and tantalizing picture of Jesus Christ as a learning teacher, there is a creative, conversational learning process that can take us further. In Part 3 we engaged in a creative quest for further insights within a frame of the Christian pedagogical imagination. Do such encounters with Christ as a learning teacher take us further into knowledge of the truth of Christ? Do they draw us closer to his love? Does the 'educationalization of theology' help the church's mission?

This postscript places a particular accent on changing our ways of talking about Christ and our pastoral actions. First, it sees him unified as teacher and saviour. Next, it outlines a new pedagogical portrait of Jesus. This is followed by some pointers on changing the way we do theology, particularly official theology. Finally, it offers some lexical proposals and pastoral precepts for a future church following a learning Christ. The ideas here are, I hope, applicable to a wide range of different churches and denominations, which could enact the vision of the learning Christ.

The learning Christ as teacher and saviour

Grasping the reality of Jesus' teaching – his intentions, methodology, learning points, and degree of success – is a crucial element in understanding his mission overall. In the Introduction, we faced the problem of two versions of Jesus having drifted away from each other. The ethical teacher and the divine saviour seem to have become mutually disconnected, with resultant missiological and hermeneutical malfunctions. If Jesus the Christ is a learning teacher, we begin to see a way back to unifying him for the church and the world. His incarnation teaches God how to be human, how to communicate with humanity, and how to accept humanity into God's self. His death is also a teaching point because when he has learnt to live and love, learnt the horror of death and suffering, he has understood humanity. His life as a learning teacher is salvific because it is full of sacramental moments that become more conspicuous when we look at him as a teacher.

There is a unity between his teaching ministry and his saving passion, a unity that exists in their joint struggle between opposed absolutes: a static definition of God and an invitation into a living, conversational being, always in dynamic collegial conversation even though changeless. Forms of struggle with which teachers engage daily – between different uses of power and authority, between intellect and will, between understanding and ignorance – are in a sense all reflections of that salvific struggle in the places where he taught and on the cross. By reuniting the teacher and the sacrifice, the prophet and the priest, we gain a different view of atonement. Salvation for us no longer needs to be a transactional arrangement focused on the cross; it can now be a grander narrative of creation, incarnation, teaching, learning and suffering, leading to transformation.

Christ is seen by Walter Brueggemann as the one who, completing the work of a long line of prophets challenging authority, has 'dismantled the dominant culture and nullified its claims'.[1] Jesus' challenge in forgiving sins is a very serious threat to the authority structures. The power to forgive, or withhold forgiveness, is a central form of social control, perhaps similar to the power to know or the right to be informed, or the qualification to teach or set up a school. In the same way that Jesus presents a challenge to 'the management of the machinery of forgiveness',[2] so also he challenges the structure of theological knowledge and the gatekeepers who control it. Knowing and following a learning Christ involves dismantling some assumptions about the way theology is done, and building faith to a different construction, since the dynamic of destroying and building is so much at the heart of Jesus' teaching and of our learning. In such a construction, creation, teaching and eschatology can be understood as a single, continuous pedagogical action by God in Christ, both teaching and learning.

A new pedagogical portrait of Jesus

If we see the cross as the ultimate divine inversion of normal power dynamics, we can look for a similar set of clues in the manner and content of his teaching, and in the church's teaching and preaching about him. In Chapter 4 we itemized what scholars have identified as being certain about Jesus and his message. Now perhaps the learning and teaching Jesus, whom we have glimpsed in this book, could be described as:

- A fiery and passionate prophet with a compelling faith in God, who taught people to expose injustice, hypocrisy and oppressive theology.
- A knowledgeable teacher who destroyed and recreated the way to interpret Scripture and discern what is right.
- A clear-sighted teacher who broke the power of oppressive internal structures of theological thought.
- A courageous teacher whose life and death was a breaking open of knowledge, understanding and love.
- A highly expressive teacher whose methods often imitated his message, careless in expansiveness, heedless of impurity.

- A learning teacher who drank deeply of his Scriptures, thought a great deal, and was teachable.
- A deeply loved teacher who inspired, challenged, transformed, scolded, protected and drew his learners to himself and to the heart of the learning Trinity.

The Christian pedagogical imagination enables us to play further with these images. Jürgen Moltmann calls for theologians to develop confessional and credal formulae, adding that universal formulae help no one as they average out meaning. He notes how new titles, such as liberator, have emerged in particular theological contexts.[3] In his own chosen titles for Christ, Moltmann uses paradox: crucified God, suffering Messiah. He explains how he believes that the death on the cross is not a refutation of Messiahship, but its 'deepest realization'.[4] Could we, then, extend Moltmann's method with newly coined titles, finding in our reading of the learning Christ some new titles that capture his paradoxical, kenotic role as educator? Learning teacher? Self-emptying fountain of knowledge? Omniscient made omnidiscent? Beloved teacher? Saving teacher, teaching saviour?

Changing the way we do theology

The educationalization of theology can be facilitated by the new framing of Christology presented in this book. The church, if it wishes to reach towards the vision of a more pedagogical theology, will be helped by re-examining its theological language and pastoral practice. Language is important because it either reveals or conceals the new insights that a pedagogical theology can bring. Pastoral practice, including the programmes of training and development for all forms of ministry, teaching, and adult theological education, is also highly relevant, as it can be either a vehicle or an obstacle to a pedagogical vision. I am interested in the emancipation of theology in ways that promote deeper understanding for all, not only for an elite.

In exploring how the church's language and practice might need to evolve, we can be guided by parallel proposals on re-engineering the church for social justice mission. In 2014, John Hull's *Towards the Prophetic Church* reflected on how the church would act if it took Christ's call to justice with full seriousness. He explored how the church's ideas about mission, evangelism and training for ministry might need to evolve. He criticized Church of England mission strategy, and other churches, for pursuing a 'church-shaped mission'.[5] Hull called for official theology and language to be reconstructed to reflect the new understanding of mission.[6]

Hull's revolutionary vision is highly pertinent to the way we could change theological language and practice towards a pedagogical theology. Jesus the teacher has been given reduced importance in official theology, little more than 'a comma in the apostles' creed',[7] and this imbalance calls for emancipation.

When churches favour a hierarchical division of labour between ministers and teachers; when they pour more resources into parish structures than into schools, universities or free-standing education programmes; and when they preach forms of theology that encourage a static and passive faith, based on an uncritical and brittle reading of the Bible, they need their theology to change. They need a new consciousness.

Educationalists can provide some of the raw materials and tools for this new consciousness. It should consist of a disciplined approach to hermeneutics; a new examination of the Bible's ambiguities, its struggle between patriarchy and freedom; a fresh awareness of the kingdom of God, its inclusivity and relevance; and an understanding of the power wielded by those who hold expert theological knowledge.

An emancipated theological education, for Hull, has two steps or moments: 'out of pain and into pain'.[8] The first pain is individual, the second is collective. Implied between them is a moment of learning. For Christian adults, there is pain in the unresolved theological questions for which they may have little language: pain in having the questions, pain in ignoring them, and pain in facing them. For many, these questions are noisy and distracting. In the churches we need to learn to overcome our fear of the pain involved in facing pain. Learning feels like pain if we are afraid of it, if we fear it might harm us or undermine our faith or relationships. How would it be if we realized that Christ the learner was there with us in the confusion? Then if we turn from that individual pain to the pain of a church that fears to engage with Jesus as a learning teacher, and needs to know and understand him in those terms, this changes our structures and priorities. Hull identified the pain of learning as a barrier. In affirming the truth of his observation, we can add fear as a further barrier to engaging in theology. The Gospels start and end with the exhortation, 'do not be afraid'. Perhaps there is another new discipline alongside Hull's prophetics: pedagogical theology, the theory and practice of fearless learning for Christian growth.

What would the future of theology and the church look like if it were enriched by the discipline of pedagogical theology?

Proposals for a church where learning matters

In a church where worship, education and communal life focus around learning from Christ the learning teacher, how would the language and actions of such a church differ from most churches today? The emancipation of knowledge involves discipline; knowing and understanding the learning Christ involves the discipline of learning a new way of doing theology. Knowledge does not mean receiving a complete set of information, it is 'the strenuous pursuit of deepening apprehension over time'.[9] Knowledge 'is a form of circulation in the veins of the Body of Christ ... the community of those from whom we can learn as we pursue this knowledge is ... as wide as creation'.[10]

In a hopeful pursuit of expectations on a future church as *discens* and *docens*, following its vocation to know Christ and follow him, here I list some brief, provocative lexical and pastoral proposals, which do no more than point the direction.

How would it be if, following through on the educationalization of theology, we redefined the lexicon of Christian ministry and practice in these ways?

- Tradition: the long-term memory of Christians, overcoming their amnesia, keeping alive the 'subversive memory of Jesus'[11] that haunts the church, its forgetful custodian.
- Gospel reading: a gift to us from the early church, a palimpsest of preaching, dispute, eyewitness accounts, myth, and loving memory.
- Preaching: exposition of what can truthfully be known about the text, distinguishing it from what is false, speculative or self-indulgent, guided by the spirit of truth in addressing the story of the listeners.
- Hermeneutics: a set of skills to be learnt, informed by knowledge of the biblical text and its context. Not a matter of individual choice. There are competent and incompetent hermeneutics.
- Prayer: spending time doing nothing with God, getting to know each other. Where a set form of words is used in prayer, getting into familiar knowledge of the words, allowing their depth to enter us.
- Training for ministry: something that all ministers do together – priests, pastors, assistants, teachers, specialist chaplains, equal in importance, in the same institutions and communities, learning with and from each other.
- Adult education: an experience of stepping out of pain and into pain, based on enquiry questions that strengthen knowledge of the Christian story but also open the mind to wider significance,[12] making theologians and creating a home for them, a theological 'habitus'.[13]
- Theologian: one who asks, of discourses on the theory and practice of faith, 'Who wants to know?' and 'Who isn't in the room?'[14] with other questions such as, 'Where do these questions and answers lead?', 'What is a helpful and growth-oriented answer for this person or group now?', 'What does a successful theological conversation lead to?' and 'How shall we picture the kingdom?'
- Eschatology: the futurity of Christians, the incompleteness of our desire for God and God's desire to know us, our desire to know each other.[15]

Building on those lexical notes, how would it be if we released the Christian pedagogical imagination through giving public consideration, in parishes, schools and training programmes, to the following precepts for pastoral practice?

- Treat our texts, symbols and rituals as treasure. Avoid turning them into magical objects, avoid oversimplification, avoid overexplanation; recognize and trust their spirit-filled, silent power to convey meaning and truth; bring out the new and old, enjoy and share their richness.
- In sermons, house groups and published study materials, teach people to be unafraid of critical theology and complexity; to transcend the pain and fear of learning; to dismantle and rebuild meanings; to love the journey and the learning Christ who accompanies us; to model fearlessness and love in learning.
- In sermons, use critical tools to break open and understand the complexity of the Gospel texts, and to enjoy it, seeing Jesus the learning teacher in context through the experience of the early church.
- Establish a higher standard of hermeneutical competence in using the Bible, and apply it in training programmes for teaching, preaching and other forms of ministry; also apply it in the formation of the church's public positions on ethical matters.
- Focus pastoral and educational effort on doing what Jesus the teacher did: leading people away from micro-monitoring of behaviour, towards seeing the big picture of God's desire for us, shifting the theological obstacles in our minds, and setting us free for the demands of the kingdom.

Pastoral implementation of precepts such as these could give practical expression to the educational economy of the church.

Conclusion

The challenge that Christ poses in all eras is to create change in people, to create, destroy and recreate our learnt models of God and of life. Present with us in the Spirit, moving in us and between us, the change he brings is a learning that we ourselves, and the world, and God, are not as we had thought. It is because of the power of the Spirit to bring change that we still have a church.

Christ is eternally the place where theology meets pedagogy. The project in this book has been to discover in Christ the meeting points between pedagogy and theology, meeting points that are too often hidden by the text of the Gospels and the practice of the church.

The fragments of a learning Christology offered here are not intended to be an alternative Christological model or a competing orthodoxy. The concept of Jesus the learning teacher is profoundly orthodox. This is the same Christ whose identity can be seen in his educational outpouring. The true marks of his church include its education and learning. His kingdom is an already existing community to which we are invited to belong, a community asking questions that challenge and transform the world; it is a sign of the Trinity in which the Father, Son and Holy Spirit pay attention to each other. It is a preparation for an eternity, in which the whole company of heaven have learnt to cry holy.

Jesus the teacher is an example to all teachers. This is not because of some inevitable and mechanistic law arising from the fact that he is Lord, but because of his pedagogical characteristics, aspects of his incarnate status as a human being. His record as a teacher is a dialectic of success and failure, as all teachers have. His teaching is also a sign of his burning core of passion for the kingdom, which caused his learners to love and remember him. In his teaching passion, he questions and challenges us to know and understand him more deeply. To those of us who are teachers and in other forms of ministry, his loving challenge puts our sense of professional responsibility and authority, our caution and control, our evasions and complicities, to shame and to flight. He comes to us with leading questions more than with propositions. As Thomas Merton put it, 'I think a man is known better by his questions than by his answers.'[16]

Notes

1 Walter Brueggemann, 1978, *The Prophetic Imagination*, Philadelphia: Fortress Press, p. 81.

2 Brueggemann, 1978, p. 83.

3 J. Moltmann, 1995, 'The confession of Jesus Christ', in J. Moltmann and J.-B. Metz, *Faith and the Future: Essays on theology, solidarity and modernity*, Maryknoll: Orbis Books, pp. 117–22, pp. 117–18.

4 J. Moltmann, 1995, 'Messianic hope in Christianity', in Moltmann and Metz, pp. 109–15, p. 112.

5 John Hull, 2014, *Towards the Prophetic Church: A study of Christian mission*, London: SCM Press, p. 236.

6 Hull, 2014, p. 207.

7 Hull, 2014, p. 200.

8 Hull, 2014, p. 248.

9 Mike Higton, 2013, 'A Theology of the University', unpublished paper for the Society for the Study of Theology, p. 2.

10 Higton, 2013, p. 4.

11 Johann Baptist Metz, 1980, *Faith in History and Society: Toward a practical fundamental theology*, London: Burns and Oates, pp. 88–9.

12 Natalie Wigg-Stevenson, 2014, *Ethnographic Theology: An inquiry into the production of theological knowledge*, New York: Palgrave Macmillan, pp. 177ff.

13 Wigg-Stevenson, 2014, pp. 47ff.

14 Rowan Williams, 2019, 'Introduction and epilogue', in Alastair Hulbert and Peter Matheson (eds), 2019, *In Your Loving is Your Knowing: Elizabeth Templeton: Prophet of our times*, Edinburgh: Birlinn Ltd, pp. 211–15, p. 211.

15 Judith Wolfe, 2014, 'Eschatology and human knowledge of God', in Anthony Clarke and Andrew Moore (eds), *Within the Love of God: Essays on the doctrine of God in honour of Paul S. Fiddes*, Oxford: Oxford University Press, pp. 157–69.

16 Thomas Merton, 1965, *Conjectures of a Guilty Bystander*, New York: Doubleday, p. 5.

Index of Bible references

Old Testament

New Testament

Index of names and subjects